Praise for *Ariise*

'Zoe has the ability to uplift and empower you.'
Turia Pitt

'*Ariise* is a profound journey of healing and transformation.
Zoe Marshall proves that even in the face of adversity,
the power of manifestation and self-belief can create
a life of purpose and joy.' **Jackie O**

'A thoughtful and empowering resource for anyone ready to
embrace manifestation.' **Lillian 'FlexMami' Ahenkan**

'Filled with wisdom and heart, *Ariise* has a unique ability
to motivate and uplift. This book is a powerful guide to
unlocking your potential.' **Sally Obermender, TV presenter
and author of *Never Stop Believing***

'*Ariise*'s insights are both profound and practical.
This book is a gift to anyone on a journey of self-discovery.'
Allyson Felix, Olympic Gold Medallist

'If you read this book, it will change your life.'
Dr Rick Hanson, author of *Buddha's Brain*

'Zoe leaves all her wisdom and heart on the pages of this
book. It's both comforting and inspiring.' **Samantha Jade,
ARIA award winning singer–songwriter**

Ariise: Manifest the life you deserve

Zoe Marshall

SIMON &
SCHUSTER

New York · Amsterdam/Antwerp · London · Toronto · Sydney · New Delhi

ARIISE: MANIFEST THE LIFE YOU DESERVE
First published in Australia in 2025 by
Simon & Schuster (Australia) Pty Limited
Level 4, 32 York St, Sydney NSW 2000

10 9 8 7 6 5 4 3 2 1

New York Amsterdam/Antwerp London Toronto Sydney New Delhi
Visit our website at www.simonandschuster.com.au

A catalogue record for this
book is available from the
National Library of Australia

NATIONAL
LIBRARY
OF AUSTRALIA

ISBN: 9781761631337

Cover design: Alissa Dinallo
Typeset by Midland Typesetters, Australia
Printed and bound in Australia by Griffin Press

MIX
Paper | Supporting
responsible forestry
FSC
www.fsc.org   FSC® C018684

The paper this book is printed on is certified against the
Forest Stewardship Council® Standards. Griffin Press holds
chain of custody certification SCS-COC-001185. FSC®
promotes environmentally responsible, socially beneficial
and economically viable management of the world's forests.

To the stars in my sky,
Ever and Fox

Contents

Introduction

You deserve
to be here

'You attract what you are, not what you want.' – James Allen

You made it. I'm humbled you chose this book. I promise, it happened for a reason. You may already know what that reason is, or perhaps you're not quite sure yet. Whether manifestation is already part of your life and you're seeking to deepen your practice, or you're a curious sceptic like I was, you are exactly where you're supposed to be.

When I sat down to write this book, I had a clear intention: This book would be a vessel for this ancient wisdom, a resource for whoever needs and deserves it. And the truth is, everyone deserves it.

If you can think and feel, you can manifest. Manifestation is our birthright, it's just that most of us don't know it!

Manifestation means different things to different people. For me it means understanding that we all have the ability to create the life we deserve. What does that mean: to deserve? It means that YOU get to choose what type of beautiful life you have, and you get to receive that life because you are worthy of it. This is not what the majority of us are taught to believe by our parents and carers.

Many misunderstand manifestation and see it as a fun little activity to play with, others think it's witchy, woo-woo, or it's just 'wishful thinking'. But to make something 'manifest' is to make it real – tangible, literal. Manifestation is the process of transforming what is *intangible* – our thoughts, dreams, wants – into the *tangible*, with support from our higher power.

I was born curious, I always knew I would have an exceptional life. A unique life. But not an easy one. I was wooed by the mystery of the world and the intangible. I had always known there was something greater than us. At the age of six, I asked my mother if I could go to scripture classes (something that perplexed her). And as I grew, I continually explored the concepts of God, religion and spirituality, trying to see where I fit in. In a way, I was trying to make sense of co-creation. And as soon as I did, I knew that I needed to share it with you.

Think of it like this: at birth you are given a guidebook for life, but every second page has been torn out. You try to live by what the book says, but without those missing pages life feels hard to understand and work through. Things always seem more challenging than they should be. And then one day you meet someone that has the *whole book*, every page. When you read it, things finally start to make perfect sense. Now you understand what this book was trying to tell you, and you are able to create the life you deserve; you feel empowered and in charge. This is manifestation.

In the pages ahead we will learn that our words – and how we choose to use them – are important to every single part of the manifestation process. And the feelings that are connected to those words are equally important to how we co-create. Language is a strange thing. When words are overused they become diluted, their meaning gets lost, and they can even at times become controversial. This is common in the wellness and self-development world, and words like *manifestation* and *universe* have become corny. And I'm totally with you if you feel that sometimes this whole industry and wellness world can all seem a little bit . . . wanky and disconnected from reality.

In this book, I will use the words *manifestation* and *universe* – and my hope is that we can fix any misconceptions you might have about these concepts – but I prefer the term 'co-creation'. This is a term I have created for both the skeptics and believers, and this is because your deliberate *intention* (what you are asking for) married with what I call *aligned action* (doing something to make it happen) is a HUGE factor in creating the life you want. You are in control. And your co-creator or collaborator in this is what I personally like to call my 'higher power', aka the universe, but you may refer to yours as God, spirit, source, or any other name which feels true to you. For me, my higher power is the universe, God, mother nature and spirit combined – and my relationship to this higher power is as important and connected to me as my marriage and my role as mother. It's the heartbeat of my co-creations and my life. Your own relationship to your higher power will be unique and individual to you, but it is essential to co-creation.

Co-creation, or manifestation, is not wishful thinking. It's not waving a magic wand (but it will feel magical at times).

Co-creation is collaborating with the universe to call in what you want by taking aligned action, mastering your mindset and deepening your ability to commit to and trust in this process.

Co-creation and manifestation are the same thing, and they are guided by the laws of the universe. The relationship between what we can and cannot influence is a subtle and nuanced element of co-creation. In my experience, it is only in the doing – through trial and error – that each of us comes to our own understanding of this nuance. This book is a modern and practical guide to help you discover that nuance and harness this ancient knowledge that science is only now beginning to understand.

This book is an invitation to create the life you deserve. And that means that it will require more than just reading. It requires both *belief* and *action*; it will require you to take a leap of faith, to be courageous at times and discover your truest self. *Ariise* asks you to explore it, to play with it, work with it, to rest with it, to heal with it, to get gritty and be audacious with it. Trust this book and yourself; it is challenging in the most exciting way possible. There will be epiphanies and there will be confronting moments. Be soft through it all. Remember you are exactly where you need to be, evolving into who you really are.

This book is going to guide and teach you how to co-create effectively and deliberately. It will also become a mirror at times – some unexpected things may come up for you during the reading process, including unhealed trauma and unprocessed emotions, and maybe even anger and frustration. This is normal and even expected. Be gentle with yourself during this self-discovery. This is necessary. Self-respect, curiosity and a willingness to explore new concepts are going to be so important as you do this work.

Together, we are going deep into the meaning of manifestation – or co-creation. We are going to see whether you are starting at rock bottom or neutral, and we are going to align our vibration with our wants. I will share tips and tools that I have found useful in my own practice. Throughout this process we will meet blocks (self-limiting beliefs) that we will learn to break through. The universe will test us at times – all for our own good – and there will be moments when we need to be uncomfortable (it will be so worth it). We're going to learn how to stop self-sabotaging and to trust the process, even when we are in the Abyss (what the hell is 'the Abyss'? Don't worry, we'll get to that). We will also learn how to maintain the momentum and motivation that co-creation requires, and how to stay accountable and committed to our practice.

Human beings are hard-wired for safety-seeking behaviours. These instincts are inherent in our DNA – they are essential to survival, so we try to avoid injury, we do what it takes to keep our jobs, our spouses, our stability. Outside of that, things seem unsafe, things are unpredictable, things are dangerous. These safety-seeking behaviours exist for a reason: they help us survive. But they can also hold us back. They stop us from asking 'What if?' Even when that nagging feeling inside us is desperate to be seen and explored, begging us to hear it, asking us: 'What do we really want?'

Tap into your *audacity*. We all deserve to be audacious. What does that word mean to you? Bravery or courage? It should! I've only come this far because of my own co-creation audacity. I am asking you to take an audacious step towards the life you deserve. Concepts in this book may feel foreign and different from what you were raised to believe and what many of those who surround you believe. But I am inviting you to manifest with great audacity.

Are you ready?

For many of us, embracing co-creation requires a major shift in perspective. It requires us to take an honest look at our lives, our habits and the way we think about ourselves and the world around us. You may hear your inner critic telling you that you're not worthy, that you're not capable, that you won't get the life you deserve. I played small for many years wanting to belong. To be accepted. It was a survival technique. But I am no longer willing to stay small for anyone in my life ever again. Even if that's at the cost of a friendship or my own comfort, so be it. This book has all the tools you need to silence that inner critic – but for these tools to work, you must make space for this process in your life. You must give this work the time, energy and care that it requires.

To do this, you must set yourself up to succeed. Some of these concepts will be very new and may take time to digest. I recommend simmering on them, questioning them, exploring them. Take time to integrate these new concepts into your life. Especially as we deconstruct parts of ourselves to make space for the new. We need time to grieve what no longer serves us.

Each chapter will include exercises, meditations, prompts or suggestions that are designed to help you get the most out of this book. I recommend using a notebook or a journal to take notes and record your thoughts and feelings as you read.

I also invite you to connect with the Ariise community – a place where you can find additional resources and like-minded people who are there to support you as you evolve on your journey. I like to think of Ariise as a movement, because the more of us who awaken to the power of co-creation, the more of us who align our vibration with the universe, the better. The Ariise community is an online space for learning, for deepening your practice, and for community and accountability (something we will return to again at the end of this book). Throughout the following chapters, there will be meditations, visualisations and other tools to assist you on your journey – but you can access Ariise online by using the QR code in the back of this book.

This work is about personal responsibility – and that includes responsibility for your mental health. If trauma is activated as you explore this work, please remember that this book is not a substitute for professional mental health advice, diagnosis or treatment. If something requires professional help, please seek it.

This work will challenge you. It will require unrelenting belief, but if you commit to this work, it will forever change you.

This is the start of something spectacular. This is the start of creating the life you deserve.

How manifestation changed my life

There's this philosophy about the human soul that I really love. It's this idea that we all get to choose our lives prior to being born, and this isn't the only life we have. We come back as many times as necessary for our souls to learn the lessons they need to learn. Looking back at my life so far, sometimes I wonder, would I maybe have chosen something a little more gentle? A smoother path? Maybe, but if I had a choice I would never give up the lessons I've learned.

I do love my life. I love my husband, my children and my home. I love my friends and my community, my work and my purpose. I love the sense of financial freedom, safety and physical well-being that I have in my life. I love the contributions I am making to the world. But it wasn't always like this. In my twenties, I was living a life that was the exact opposite of the one I've just described, an awful life and existence. I hit rock bottom: I was purely surviving, constantly in a state of dread and fear. But to understand how I hit that rock bottom I have to take you back much, much further. I need to tell you about my mother.

I was born to the most amazing woman. My mother was told she would never have children, so when I was born I was raised as her 'miracle' child. No pressure! My mum taught me many great things. Unconditional love was one of them. She was the most open-minded and non-judgemental person you could ever meet. From a young age, I enjoyed asking her incredibly curious and controversial questions, always exploring where the boundaries were. I remember asking her whether she would mind if I became a prostitute someday. I was ten and didn't understand what that meant, but I knew it was edgy and wanted to learn more. Mum, who was never fazed by my curiosity, said, 'You can be anything you want when you grow up, as long as you don't hurt people.' She was the wisest and kindest person I've ever known.

Mum was always spiritual, leaning towards the teaching of Buddha, but she was open to pretty much everything. She would read our horoscopes from the newspaper on a Sunday morning over cream cheese and salmon bagels (when we could afford them). She had my birth chart done when I was born.

She was also that person others would turn to in crisis, the person who held our family unit together, someone who offered tenderness to every person she met. She gave those around her all the time in the world. She was present, and she relished in others' presence.

When I was growing up, my mum and I were very close; it was us against the world. We were so close that my therapist used the word *enmeshed* to describe our relationship. And although that enmeshment came with many challenges, I wouldn't change a thing. My dad was a drummer and Mum was a model when they met at just seventeen. They travelled around Europe, living and working like the young rockstars they were. But my parents split when I was three. The story I was told was that Mum wanted to settle down and find stability while Dad still wanted to keep living that rockstar life. Mum looked after me the majority of the time and I saw Dad every second weekend. Those weekends with Dad were a struggle for both of us and I experienced debilitating separation anxiety whenever I was away from my mum.

Dad was around sparingly, and that was just physically rather than emotionally. It was Mum who was really there for me, all day every day. She raised me (with the help of my nan – her mum). I was an only child, so my mum and I dealt with the ups and downs of life together, it was always just the two of us. The problem with enmeshment is that because we relied only on each other, we developed a co-dependency that challenged my ability to step into adulthood. I wasn't fully prepared and empowered to face what was to come in the big bad world. And this would cause major problems for me in the years to come.

Mum also worked incredibly hard. Nothing was easy for her. She grew up watching her father beat her mother, and at eleven she insisted that her own mum leave her dad. She was fiercely brave, even as a child. In a way, my mum became the parent figure in that moment and she played that role for my nan for the rest of her life. I can't fathom what an extraordinary responsibility that was. But my mum was determined to break the cycle. She was adamant that she wouldn't carry on that generational trauma, and she didn't – my dad was never violent or emotionally abusive to my mother.

It's so strange. It was as if I knew from a very young age what was coming. I knew in my gut it wouldn't last. I knew I wouldn't have her for long. That no one got to experience this level of supreme unconditional love forever. I used to lie awake at night scared that she would die. I would ask her to promise that she would never leave me. I only felt safe in the world if she was a part of mine.

As I grew up, finished high school, and entered my twenties, our inseparable bond was always there, my own personal safety net. And then one day, Mum came into the kitchen and as we stood at the sink she told me that the doctors had found a lump in her breast – 5 centimetres in diameter. She had already had a biopsy and we were awaiting the results. It's wild how something so small can change your whole world. In that moment, it felt as if I dissociated: I couldn't hear or see properly, everything went fuzzy. And I just knew in my gut that she would die. I would lose her.

Not long after her diagnosis, my mum asked me to watch a DVD a friend had loaned her. It was called *The Secret*, based on the book by Rhonda Byrne. Everyone was talking about it, circulating the DVD and sharing extracts from the book. It went viral long before going viral was even a thing. By this time, Mum was truly fighting her cancer, and I think that was the reason her friend had loaned the DVD in the first place: there was a scene in *The Secret* about someone who had cured their own cancer. We both felt hopeful, even though I was very confused. We watched the film and I remember looking at my mum at the end and asking, 'What's the secret?' The concept was way too big for me at that time. What the hell was the 'Law of Attraction'? What did 'manifestation' even mean?!

I didn't have time to find out. The next month, my mum died. I have no words to explain the experience of losing her. For a long time, I was in denial. In some ways I still am. I don't know if my little heart will ever really believe she's gone. I still have these horrific dreams where she's left me without explaining where she's gone or when she will be back. I try to call and she doesn't answer, or the phone disconnects when she does. In some dreams we make a plan to meet and she never turns up, I just wander around the streets calling her name like a little child desperately trying to find their parent in a busy shopping centre. Anyone who has experienced the deep grief from the loss of a loved one knows exactly what I'm talking about.

Without my mum, I was scared, I felt untethered, and I didn't have anyone to save me, no one was there for me – not even God or the universe. I felt abandoned. If there was a God, why would they do this? My mum was my only safe haven, and without her the world had become a very dangerous and isolating place.

Mum and I had shared everything with each other but I had kept one very big secret from her. It was a secret I was keeping from everybody.

The truth was that I had been in a very violent and dangerous relationship with a man. This person had promised to love and protect me, but instead I endured physical and sexual violence as well as the emotional and psychological violence we now call coercive control. As anyone who has experienced domestic violence knows, abusive relationships can turn us into someone we never imagined we'd become. Abusers have clever strategies for isolating and gaslighting their victims, and this can have a profound effect on the way we see ourselves and the world.

Shortly after my mother's death, while I was still in this very dangerous relationship, my extended family imploded. It was another challenge that proved me right in my belief that the world was a cruel place. It even proved my partner right: that without my mum, I only had him.

Weird things happen when someone dies. People handle their grief in strange ways. My own memories of this time are clouded by grief and abuse. And now that so many years have also passed, it's difficult to separate facts from feelings. I'm sure that everyone involved has their own very different version of events – each version coloured by their own trauma and grief. But this is how that time felt for me.

As I have shared, my mum had become nan's support system when she was just eleven years old, and this care and responsibility only grew as my nan aged and became more and more dependent on her daughter. So, when Mum died, my nan and her other children – my aunt and uncle – felt just as lost as I did. My mum was the glue that held my family together. And now that she was gone, my extended family was holding me responsible for mum's financial obligations – obligations I didn't have the means to fulfill. My nan, who had helped raise me, funneled her grief into getting financial safety from the very little money mum had left behind when she died.

And it got really rough. I was treated like a stranger, a business associate rather than the grieving daughter, granddaughter or niece. Instead of family gatherings to mourn together and grieve my mum, there were court cases and lawyers. It was the worst time of my life.

Looking back on it now, I understand that everyone involved was acting out of desperation and their own complicated grief. They weren't thinking about the long-term damage and impact on me or our relationship. At that time, they were trying to survive their own loss. I know that people can do terrible things – things they wouldn't normally do – when they're grieving. I also know that my family did the best they could at the time. Did it mess me up? Yes. Did it force me to sink even deeper into the disgusting relationship I was in, as a deranged form of survival? Yes. Would others have forgiven this betrayal? Probably not. But my mother raised me to forgive, and to try and see everyone's perspective.

This isn't easy to write. It's hard to go back to these places as I share my story with you. It's vulnerable to share our wounds – even if they have healed.

But it wasn't over yet. I still hadn't hit my rock bottom. While all of this family trauma was unfolding, I depended even more on my abusive partner. And he controlled everything in my life. It got to the point that the only safe place was inside my mind – my thoughts were the only thing he didn't have access to. He controlled where I went, how I dressed, what I ate, what I did and who I spoke to – I wasn't allowed to be on social media. And breaking his rules would start a violent episode. The only safe activity I was allowed was reading.

This wasn't threatening to him, and he never showed any interest in what I was reading. Books were safe. No one was looking at me or touching me while I was reading a book. I couldn't run away with a book. Reading was a 'good girl' activity. And, even though I was in a hopeless place, my deepest knowing led me to books about self-development, manifestation, co-creation and the power of our thoughts.

Ironically, my ex was the one who gave me the book that would finally give me the strength to leave. A friend had lent him Neale Donald Walsch's *Conversations with God*. My ex considered himself a religious person – which, considering his horrific behaviour, isn't very on brand – and he thought he was giving me a book about God. Little did he know that it is a book about spiritual truth, finding your highest self . . . *and* about relationships.

I started to ask myself questions, exploring the parts of me that were buried underneath the rubble of abuse, to see what I believed about myself, to really listen to the way I spoke to myself *about* myself. I began to examine my sense of self-worth, how much I valued myself and if I had any self-respect left after what I had been through. I began to ask the most diffi-cult question of all: How did I get here? And during this time of self-examination – while I was so desperate for a life with less pain, less hurt, less fear – I began to seek answers, healing and a new way of living. I wanted to relearn and change the way that I approached . . . *everything*.

I managed to leave my abusive relationship, but I wasn't completely free from its grip. And it's hard to know if I would ever have put all of this new learning into action if it hadn't been for what happened next. After yet another violent episode with my ex, I was driving angry and upset in the rain when I lost control of the car.

I genuinely thought I was going to die. But when I crawled out of the wreckage, the first thing I did was reach for my phone, which had been flung across the road. I wasn't trying to call an ambulance, or even my dad. The person I called in that moment was my abusive partner: the same man who I had been trying to get away from when I crashed. It's hard to acknowledge that level of insanity when I look back. As the paramedics put me in a neck brace and back brace, worried that I might have internal and spinal injuries, all I could think about was him being mad at me.

When he arrived at the crash site I was still being worked on in the ambulance. Later, at the hospital, he told me that if I hadn't driven off upset, I would still be safe at home with him. He told me there was no point calling my family.

'Nobody cares about you. I'm all you've got,' he said. And I believed him. I had no money, no car, and I was stuck in a brace.

It was the lowest low point in my life, and I didn't have my mum or family to help me through it. There were many times during this period of immense pain when I questioned my relationship with my higher power, asking myself: If the universe truly loved and supported me, then how did I find myself here? It was only in retrospect that I understood that this was a lesson my soul needed to learn.

What I realised after the crash was that I really *could* have died. And I had been suffering immensely, I was isolated from my friends and family, I was stuck in a cycle of abuse – and I wanted so much more than that. I knew there was more to life than this. So I slowly found the strength to leave my toxic relationship for good. The lengthy legal and financial conflicts with my extended family eventually came to an end and we were able to make amends. It was only then, when I wasn't in survival mode, when I had some space and safety, that I began to fully grieve the loss of my mother and face the trauma that I had endured. I did many years of confronting work to heal, so that now her memory brings joy, even though there will always be longing.

Ariise

I felt it was important to share this with you as we start this co-creation experience. It's important for me that you witness my rock bottom, and how far I've come since. There is no way I would have found the deep connection to my higher power without that experience. The depths of loss and grief that I endured was integral to this work, and I can only share this knowledge with you because I survived that.

Rock bottom broke me wide open so I could receive the wisdom and knowledge that had been there all along – that is there for all of us. In a way, rock bottom is a gift. You become very open to exploring things that you completely shut down before. There's a reason that Google searches for 'manifesting' went up by 600% during Covid.[1] People felt trapped, stuck, lost, and they were finally open to explore alternative ways to thrive.

Your highest self already knows how to co-create or manifest, and it innately understands that the universe wants to support us all towards living our greatest lives. I believe it, because I've lived it.

As we move through this work together, I will share with you some of my experiences with co-creation or manifestation: the good, the bad and the ugly. Because sometimes our inner critics are brutal and this work can feel challenging, it can seem easier to give up. We see evidence that the world is a hostile place, and it can be hard to see it as the loving place that it truly is, full of infinite possibilities. I hope that this book will help you see the truth: that the universe is always working with us, not

---

1   Stuart McGurk, 'Making dreams come true: Inside the new age world of manifesting', *The Guardian*, 20 March 2022.

against us. And I'm telling you this as someone who lost herself while battling an abusive relationship when her mother was dying of cancer.

When I finally saw enough evidence to break my own scepticism, I could look back at that traumatic time and see all the important lessons that I needed to learn and how far I'd come.

In the next chapter, we'll get into what exactly manifestation is (and what it isn't). But before we do, it's important to make a commitment. I'm asking you to make a promise. A vow to yourself, that anchors you to your purpose.

> **Zoe's Commitment:** *I am worthy of this process. I am already co-creating the life I deserve.*
>
> **My commitment:**...
> ....
>
> If it feels right, you can use my commitment – but I encourage you to write your own if you can. This could feel unfamiliar and awkward for you, but that's just a little block. Ask yourself what promise you need to make to yourself in order to set yourself up for success with this work, and then write it down as a sign of your commitment.

I see you. Because I was you. If no one has told you, or if you've never believed it, let me tell you right now: you are deserving and worthy of the life you want. Are you ready to Ariise?

Part 1

The fundamentals of co-creation

S eeing is believing. I remember so clearly the first time I really got what co-creation was, when I really *felt* it, when I saw the evidence of it right in front of my eyes.

It was the early days right after I got the courage to leave my abusive relationship. I was still so broken. My wounds were wide open, and I had so much healing to do. This was a really hard time. Wading through trauma was exhausting and scary and it felt like it would never end. One moment I was feeling happy, and then I would be blindsided with horrible memories of the abuse that I needed to acknowledge before I could move on.

But I was safe and hopeful, and I had *left*. I knew how lucky I was to leave alive. Many women don't. I was able to finally catch my breath and think about what I might actually need to start this healing journey.

And just when I needed a sign from the universe, I was invited to stay with my Godmother – my mum's best friend, Annie – in Byron Bay. Annie is family to me, and I was very honest with her about what I'd just lived through. I told her that I knew I needed help to heal, but I wasn't sure where to get it. While I was staying in Byron I visited one of my mum's friends, Liesel, and her beautiful family. Liesel was a facilitator at a very alternative retreat where people went for deep self-exploration and healing, and she thought it might be just what I needed. As soon as she described it, my heart leapt. I felt instantly that it was where I needed to be.

Retreats aren't cheap, and I didn't have access to cash after the family court case and setting up my life again after leaving my ex. But Annie kindly lent me the money and I booked my stay. Without knowing what I was in for, I went with an open yet broken heart and mind. It was everything I needed it to be. This retreat was not for the faint-hearted, and it involved lots of cathartic sharing sessions, screaming and punching into mattresses, heaving with tears. But I realised that I was desperate for this type of release. I left with what I had gone for, my healing was in motion. And I had found myself again.

Manifestation or co-creation was still new to me at this time. But without knowing it, I had already started to understand its major principles. I had identified what I needed to heal and then I'd taken action by sharing what I needed emotionally and seeking financial help from Annie. It was a classic case of 'ask and you shall receive', with the universe magnetically attracting me to the exact retreat that I needed to attend. I had co-created *subconsciously*. When I finally learned to consciously co-create, my whole life changed. Everything in my life today is the result of co-creation.

But before I can share with you some of the frameworks I use, it's important that we're all on the same page about the basics of manifestation.

Co-creation

As we have already touched on, manifestation or co-creation is the practice of collaborating with the universe to turn your dreams and wants into reality. And 'manifestation' and 'co-creation' are just two ways of referring to this work.

I prefer the term co-creation because it reminds me that I have power in the process. You are welcome to use manifestation if that feels more true for you. Whatever you choose to call it, this is a collaboration between you and your higher power (the universe, God, spirits, etc.), and it requires a lot of trust.

Some people think manifestation works like prayer. They simply ask their higher power to transform their desires and dreams into reality and then they walk away, hoping that their higher power will do all the heavy lifting. This is not how it works. And thinking about it this way is, in fact, disempowering. Wishing that your higher power will gift you with things you want is a bit like a spoilt child demanding a treat. It doesn't work like this. You are essential in this process, and you're just as powerful as the universe when you co-create.

Using the term co-creation reminds us that we are collaborating with the universe in what I will sometimes refer to as 'the work' or 'practice' – co-creation isn't passive, it requires us to take what is called 'aligned action'. This is what is so empowering about this practice: it's a partnership. It's beautiful when we realise that we have a partner in this work, and that this partner is infinite, benevolent and always working for our greater good, whether we believe it yet or not. Co-creation requires us to match the energy that the universe is bringing to this process – like any good partnership, it thrives when both partners put in effort and energy. *This* is co-creation.

But it's also important to note here that because co-creation is about our relationship with the universe, we cannot co-create for other people. We don't have control over other people's abilities and minds (although this is not to say that we don't *influence* people), and because of this we cannot co-create someone else's life. Even if we think we know what's best for someone else, or we see their potential, it doesn't necessarily mean that what we want for them is the same as what they want for themselves.

It can be tricky when it seems like the changes we want to make or the lives we want to create can't happen until other people get on board – including our family members, friends and colleagues, our community and even our politicians. As the saying goes, true change starts within. And while you can inspire others with your own positive change, you can't make them change themselves.

The opposite is also true: nobody else can do this work for you. So much of co-creation is about personal responsibility. No one is coming to save you – but, when you are truly in alignment with the universe, you won't need them to. You will save yourself.

It can be hard to hear that, as adults, we are responsible for creating our own reality. And it can feel especially confronting to realise that the lives we are living right now are the result of what our past selves believed – whether rightly or wrongly – that we deserved. Just let that sink in for a second. Your current reality is shaped by the thoughts and feelings you were having in the past. That doesn't mean that you are to blame for all the bad things that have happened to you. What it means is simply that your past beliefs have played a role in where you are today – for better or for worse. And the good news is that this work will teach you to be more aware of those beliefs so that you can use them to create the life you deserve. There's so much freedom and power in understanding that you are in the driver's seat and you don't need anyone else to create the life you want. *You* are the creator! You and the universe.

Let's turn now to the major principles that form the foundation of co-creation: the Law of Attraction, Intention, and Beliefs and Core Values.

The Law of Attraction

The Law of Attraction is a concept that has been around for a while. You may have first heard of this idea from books like *The Secret* or from the work of Esther and Jerry Hicks. However, our thinking on the Law of Attraction has had a much-needed glow-up since then, and we now have a new way for really understanding how to work with this principle.

The Law of Attraction suggests that the thoughts that we focus on are connected with the emotions we feel, and together they shape the reality we experience. The universe responds to the energy we are putting out into the world, whether consciously or unconsciously, and it gives us more of the kind of energy we're putting out.

The key concepts of the Law of Attraction include:

Like Attracts Like: Expect bad things; bad things happen. Expect great things; great things happen. The idea here is that how you think, feel and act influences what you attract into your life: positive thoughts and feelings attract positive outcomes, while negative thoughts and feelings only attract more negativity.

Energy and Vibration: Wherever you direct your energetic focus and effort puts you in a specific vibration or frequency, and the universe responds to this by sending you more of whatever is in your vibration, good or bad.

Alignment: Alignment is when your energy matches the vibration of the thing you want to create. In other words, it's when the energy you're putting out into the universe is 'aligned' with what you hope to receive in return.

Gratitude: Gratitude is the feeling of thankfulness, a kind of deep appreciation for what you have and for what you know is on its way. Learning to feel gratitude for those things that we haven't manifested yet – a mental and vibrational framework I will teach you – is a key variable in this work.

We can think of the Law of Attraction as a delicious recipe – a cup of energy, a teaspoon of gratitude – that forms the bond between you and the universe as you co-create. Just as the law of gravity manages the relationship between our bodies and the earth, the Law of Attraction is the relationship between our desires and the universe. When we put out positive energy into the world, we are asking for the universe to give us more of the same.

But does that mean we can attract and manifest bad things? This is one of the most important questions I'm asked. Let me be very clear: you can only co-create once you've learned the process. There is no such thing as accidental manifestation. All manifestations require deliberate intention, aligned action, and trust. That's why our intrusive thoughts and worries don't just turn into reality (thank God!), the same way wishing for a million dollars won't make it instantly appear. You must be the 'co' in co-creation. Actively participating in the process.

So, can you manifest bad things? Technically, yes, but why would you want to? Manifesting something negative would mean fully committing to co-creating it and trusting that this bad thing . . . is for your highest good? The very idea of manifesting pain or suffering for yourself is nonsensical. The universe is constantly working for you and with you for your highest good, and this doesn't include calling in harm, trauma or suffering.

But if we believe that the Law of Attraction is always at work and that like attracts like, it can make us wonder: can we attract negative things if we are in a negative frame of mind? Yes, this is possible – but it's not as simple as that. If you aren't harnessing the power of co-creation, then life is simply happening to you, you are not manifesting it. You might have experienced a time where you were in a negative frame of mind and bad things seemed to happen constantly, which in turn contributed to a negative mindset, forming a loop. This can absolutely happen, but it's not the same as co-creating negativity.

Co-creation is about learning how to move through pain and heal, how to move from disempowerment to empowerment, and how to actively participate in co-creating the life you deserve. This process is reclaiming your agency, no matter what you've experienced in the past.

Intention

Like manifestation, the word intention has been so overused and misunderstood that it's easy to disregard it as meaningless. Understanding what it means to be *intentional* is key to this work, however, it's vital we redefine it and reclaim this powerful tool.

A great way to understand what intention means is to understand its opposite, or 'shadow side'. The shadow side of intention is *purposelessness, accident, uncertainty* and *powerlessness.*

The opposite of intention is the idea that things just happen to us, and that we are always on the receiving end of events and experiences that we have no control over. A caveat: There are many things that we don't have control over (including other people and the weather!), but when we have deliberate intentions we influence so much more of our life than we know.

Intention is about being mindful and focused, and taking aligned action toward what you truly want. This is very different to mindless, reactionary wanting that most of us are used to. You might see an ad for ice cream that triggers a craving. And part of this is biological – we need to eat to survive – but we don't need to eat *ice cream* to survive. We are reacting to great marketing as it hits our brain and promises us all the nostalgia, comfort and pleasure that eating ice cream will bring. We also have evidence that in the past eating ice cream made all those things true. But before we even check in with ourselves to find out if we really need the ice cream, we are already buying and eating it!

Are we being puppeteered or are we making a deliberate choice? Asking ourselves this question changes the way we act on this want. Being intentional creates awareness: we can check in with ourselves about why we want what we want. Is ice cream the thing that our highest self really desires? It may be – ice cream is great! But it might also be the case that the clever marketing sucked us in.

It's no different from the way beauty and fashion brands can make us feel less than – not pretty enough or skinny enough – unless we buy the lipstick or the shapewear. We can end up letting the world around us tell us what to want. And this spills into other areas – if we aren't intentional, we might just end up studying to become a doctor because we think it will impress our family, or we might end up marrying someone we don't really love because society says it's time to tie the knot. But when we practise being intentional, we can make more intuitive and informed decisions about whether to buy that ice cream, become a doctor, or marry that man.

Lots of people fall into work that doesn't fulfill them or feel purposeful. We might blindly follow the footsteps of a family member, or choose a job simply because it was convenient or had a decent salary. But if there is no *deliberate intention* behind our choice, we won't find the work satisfying and fulfilling. Instead, we need to ask ourselves amazing questions like, 'What will feed my soul?'

The greatest question you will ever ask yourself is: 'What do I want?' Have you ever truly questioned what you want and why you want it? This might be a time to explore what true success really looks like to you rather than reacting to what society says success is. This clarity creates intention.

When you start this work, you will begin to gather information about who you really are, and it can change everything – it will even shake your very foundations if they haven't served you. It's incredible how different things can be when we live a life of deliberate intention, as opposed to a life of purposelessness and powerlessness where we go where the wind blows. When we discover our true wants and act on them with intention, we begin to feel a sense of purpose, passion and drive, and it has a tremendous impact on our sense of satisfaction.

You can start this anytime, anywhere – it is never too late to begin the process of deliberately, intentionally living your life.

SET YOUR INTENTION

What exactly does the life you dream of look like? Let's practise setting an intention.

Open your journal or turn to the blank pages at the back of this book and let your wildest hopes and dreams flow through you without judgement. Now here's the trick: write about this new life *as if* you already have it. It might look something like this:

'*I create beautiful art that allows me to make a comfortable income, I own my home that has a beautiful veggie garden, I choose what to do with my time everyday and I choose to move my body, make nourishing meals, connect with loving friends. I have met my wonderful life partner and we have started a family.*'

Now that this beautiful new life is in front of your eyes, you can get a clear idea of what you really want and how it might feel to have it.

You can take this as far as you like, the sky is the limit. Reflecting on the commitment you made in the previous chapter and remembering that you are supported and ready to receive will anchor this all in place. This is how you create the life you deserve.

Beliefs and Core Values

When you hear the word 'belief', what comes to mind? Which concepts and ideas do you consider to be your beliefs? For lots of us, beliefs refer to religious or spiritual perspectives. They can also be things we consider to be true about the nature of the universe, or spirit or God, or whatever name you choose to use. For others, our beliefs may be based in science or academia, or on the evidence we've collected through our life experiences. Many beliefs come from how we were raised and what we heard, watched and were exposed to when we were little.

Beliefs are not the same as facts. Facts rely on objective data and require 'hard evidence' to verify, while beliefs often rely on faith and more subjective feelings or intuition. However, not all belief systems are good or positive. Racism, sexism and other types of bigotry are also belief systems. Sometimes, the beliefs that impacted previous generations are passed down to us and we inherit beliefs that no longer serve us.

We are inundated with belief systems that tell us how we should see ourselves, each other and our place in the world. Sometimes we might not know what our beliefs are until we sit with ourselves and really think about it. But it is worth thinking about, because our beliefs are very powerful things, and they will influence what the universe sends our way.

It's also important to know that our beliefs will continue to change as our lives evolve. For example, when I hit rock bottom there was a time when I lost faith in my higher power. This belief changed again after I had healed. It's completely normal for beliefs to evolve.

FYI

Our beliefs are powerful. The placebo effect is a well-documented neurological phenomenon that highlights the power of belief and positive thinking on our experiences of reality. The most common example of the placebo effect is in medical trials, when a small group of patients known as a control group is given medication without any active ingredients, while another group receives the real deal. There is a large body of evidence that shows that patients who are given a placebo – a decoy pill with no real pharmaceutical benefit – often still report feeling better. Why? Because they *believed* that they were getting better, and their minds and bodies responded to this belief.

But the placebo effect goes beyond medical trials. A 2017 study published in *Scientific Reports* scanned the brains of thirty participants as they were given small samples of wine and asked to give it a taste rating. Before the participants took a sip, they were informed of the price of the bottle. Only, they weren't told the real prices – they were given made up prices to test the hypothesis: Does our belief that a wine is more costly make it taste better? As it turns out, it does.[2] Our minds are so powerful! Simply believing that a wine is more expensive is enough for our physical experience of taste and enjoyment to be amplified. Imagine what we can do when we harness this ability and use it to focus on our goals?

As we have learned, the Law of Attraction is about similar energies or 'vibes' attracting each other. If you are confident

---

2   Lisa Schmidt *et al*, 'How context alters value: The brain's valuation and affective regulation system link price cues to experienced taste pleasantness' *Scientific Reports* 7 (2017).

and have the audacity to co-create what you truly want, and you believe you are worthy of it, that resonates with the universe and you become a magnet for that energy. The universe knows that you are worthy (whether you truly believe it yet or not) and it knows how to support you in turning thoughts and feelings into things. The trick is you also need to match this energy to the positive frequency of the universe, and to what you want to call into your life. This is what I refer to as *aligning your vibe*.

There's a quote I love that is often attributed to Mahatma Gandhi: 'A man is but the product of his thoughts. What he thinks, he becomes.' When you lack belief in yourself and what you can achieve, everywhere you turn you will see evidence of things not working out. You will see barriers instead of bridges, closed doors instead of open ones, and enemies instead of allies. But when you believe in your abilities and have self-worth, you send that confident energy out into the universe and it will bounce it right back in the form of opportunities!

If beliefs are habits of thought and mental frameworks that influence our expectations and outcomes, then what are core values? We understand what *values* are – they are the moral and ethical (perhaps spiritual or religious) frameworks through which we make sense of the world around us, and that can help us to make decisions and choices.

Our *core* values refer to those fundamental values that are non-negotiable, that are central to who we are and how we understand the world and our place in it. These are the values that we return to when we're presented with a challenge, or when we are checking in with ourselves to make sure that our choices and actions are in alignment with the person we want to be.

As obvious as this sounds, many of us never actually take the time to identify precisely what our core values are. Taking time to go inwards and be deliberate about our core values is not only a good practice for life, but also vital to co-creation. Finding this clarity will help you as you learn to set goals and intentions.

But how do we work out what our core values actually are?

Journaling can be a great way of discovering what really matters to you. As you write down your thoughts, look back over what you've written and highlight the recurring themes that stand out to you: if you're hyper-focused on your career, perhaps ambition is something you value? And if you find yourself writing most often about your family and friends, you might be someone who really values community. Do you write down lots of ideas for making art, music, or poetry? That might be a sign that you value creativity.

Another great way to uncover your core values is to think back to the values you were raised with, and how they shaped you. Did your parents instill in you a sense of fairness whenever your argued with a friend or sibling? Was honesty always the best policy in your house growing up? Write down the values you were raised with, and then consider if these are things you still live by, or whether they are outdated and need to evolve.

If journalling and exploring how you were raised aren't providing the insight you were hoping for, try looking a little further. Who are the people in your life, in your community, and even in the media that you admire? What values do these people project: is it compassion, courage, generosity, humility? As you think about these inspiring people, consider what impact you want to have on those close to you, on your wider community, and even on the world. How would you like to be described if you weren't in the room? These are all great ways to pinpoint what really matters to you.

Take some time now to write a list of your core values in your journal or on the blank pages at the back of this book. Discuss your core values with the people in your life that you most trust and admire, and show curiosity towards discovering what their core values are. It's helpful to choose no more than six core values, so that you can really come to know them intimately and weave them into your co-creation practice. Remember, you can have as many values as you want, but think of your *core values* as the sun – everything else revolves around them. Here are a few that may stimulate your thinking:

Achievement	Justice	Empathy
Ambition	Kindness	Growth
Beauty	Learning	Inclusion
Community	Lightness	Innovation
Compassion	Love	Loyalty
Courage	Optimism	Mindfulness
Creativity	Persistence	Reliability
Discipline	Playfulness	Responsibility
Equality	Purpose	Sustainability
Expression	Respect	Trust
Flexibility	Service	Wisdom
Fun	Simplicity	Gratitude
Generosity	Vision	Adventure
Honesty	Accountability	Health
Humility	Authenticity	Selflessness
Individuality	Balance	
Integrity	Courage	

As you become more deliberate and familiar with your core values, I encourage you to reflect on how they show up in your day-to-day activities, commitments, interactions with others, and in how you treat yourself. Start to notice the places where your core values are not as present as you'd like them to be. Visualise what your life would look like if your activities, habits and experiences were always in the highest possible alignment with your core values. What would that make you feel like? Does it inspire a sense of joy, of happiness, of empowerment?

If you want something just because of status, ego or what someone else will say or think . . . it won't materialise in the way that you want, because it doesn't align with your core values. There is an honesty and purity to co-creation, and this is because the universe is honest and pure. This requires us to ask ourselves hard questions about why we want something, and to learn to identify when our ego is at work. If you want a red Ferrari because your mates will think you're cool, then the whole process is being run by ego – this is not the kind of energy we need when we're co-creating. Ego-driven energy is resistant and competitive, and super icky. If you want a red Ferrari because it's going to allow you a sense of freedom, ease, joy – because when you visualise driving it you feel a sense of wellbeing and excitement – then you've tapped into a reason that is aligned with your core values, and your manifestation will flow effortlessly and with ease.

It's important to note, however, that 'effortlessly and with ease' does not necessarily mean that it will manifest instantly. In fact, rarely does this happen. This is because co-creation works with its own divine timing. It's not a genie in a lamp. It can't make something out of nothing! So, as impatient as we are (and trust me, I am the most impatient person I know) we can't pressure the universe to give us what we want immediately, like a petulant child demanding a treat. That demanding and impatient vibration is repellent to the universe, and it won't help with receiving your co-creations. So, get honest and reflect on your core values as you begin to set intentions.

Beliefs and core values are not the same thing, but the two can work together. Our beliefs often inform our value system. And our values can also influence our beliefs. But they are different, and they don't always align. Let's say that one of your core values is kindness – you value kindness in others and try to be a kind person yourself. But, because of negative experiences in your past, deep down you may still believe that the world is not a kind place, that most other people are unkind. This will send a very confusing message to the universe! Instead of bringing the kindness that you value into your life, it is likely to attract more unkindness. So, to break down that old belief, you need to look for evidence of a different belief, one that supports your core value of kindness. What evidence can you see in the world of the kindness of others? Take notice when a stranger gives you a compliment, or when someone takes the time to help you at work. Build up evidence that will support a new belief: that the world is full of kindness.

As I have said, our beliefs are not set in stone. They are dynamic, they are changeable, and they are ours to design and control. It is true that some people are born into privilege while others are not, and this can have a major impact on our lives and our 'starting point' when it comes to so much of what we are exploring in these pages. But it is also true that we can change our beliefs, we can change our mental and emotional frameworks and we can change our core values.

It's very important that your core values and beliefs align. Because belief is *the* essential part of co-creation. I would go so far as saying that without it, there's no point moving forward. Belief is what aligns your thoughts, emotions and actions with what you want to manifest. For co-creation to work, it requires your trust and faith. Attempting to manifest something without truly believing it is possible sends a confusing sign to the universe – and yourself!

This can be a challenging step in the process, especially for those of us who have lived within a belief system that tells us there is lack and scarcity, and that things like abundance, wealth, success and health, are for other people but not for *us*. If this is you, that's okay. It's more common than you think. In fact, I would say that most people have some really unhelpful unconscious belief systems, and it's completely natural that this work will bring up some old habits and patterns that require us to heal and evolve.

FYI

In so many ways, our bodies were designed for co-creation. Our brains have this very cool thing called a Reticular Activating System, or RAS. The RAS is a group of nerves in our brainstem – located just behind our eyes – and its purpose is filtering the information we receive through our senses. It's responsible for keeping us focused on what's important and filtering out what's not. Studies have shown that our brains cannot process all the information we receive through our senses, and that we actually filter most of it out.[3] The RAS helps to draw our attention to the things that matter to us: it's

---

3   Wiliam, Dylan, 'The Half Second Delay: What Follows?' Pedagogy, Culture & Society, Vol. 14, No. 1, March 2006, p. 71.

why, when you decide that you want to fall pregnant you suddenly start noticing pregnant women everywhere you go. It's not that they weren't there before, it's just that your RAS was filtering them out – until they became significant to you.

You might have also heard of something called 'confirmation bias', and that works in a similar way to our RAS. When we hold a particular belief, we tend to pay *much* more attention to evidence that supports our belief, to the point that we might even discount anything we see or hear that goes against it. In other words, we filter out anything that doesn't confirm our belief – just like the RAS filters out information that doesn't seem significant. This can be both a blessing and a curse, depending on what beliefs we hold. For example, if we believe that the world is a hostile place and people are out to get us, we might misinterpret someone who is genuinely trying to help us as a threat – we may assume that a friendly stranger offering to help us carry our shopping is actually trying to rob us! On the flipside, if we hold positive beliefs – for example, that good things are always on the horizon – we'll be more inclined to look out for positive signs and recognise good things when they come our way.

As we continue on this journey, we'll be learning how to retrain our brains to look for new, more positive data – data that affirms our positive beliefs.

Myths and Misunderstandings

Now, be honest. As you've read and absorbed the information here, have you found yourself feeling doubtful, sceptical, maybe even a little annoyed or frustrated? There's a reason for that. I have a few problems with *The Secret* and teachings like it.

These teachings offer some valuable information but they also perpetuate certain myths and misunderstandings that cause many people to turn away from this work. Let's examine these myths and misunderstandings more closely, so that we may leave them behind and replace them with better understanding.

Myth: *Co-creation is a 'set and forget' process. All we have to do is ask for something, and it will arrive.*	**Truth:** Asking is a fundamental part of the process, it's true. But we must also take aligned action by using some of the emotional and behavioural tools that we will explore in this book.
Myth: *There is no room for being doubtful or sceptical.*	**Truth:** Co-creation does not require that we 'dumb ourselves down' or blindly believe. It is not a religion, and it's not judging you. Sceptism is healthy. Sit with your doubts and investigate them – working through your sceptical thoughts is the best way to strengthen your beliefs.
Myth: *We must always feel good, or we can mess it all up with one 'negative' thought.*	**Truth:** Practising co-creation doesn't mean we cannot experience the full range of human emotion. For example, there are moments where anger, fear or sadness are appropriate and useful. These emotions are vital to processing big life events or personal traumas. And when we do experience these feelings, the universe doesn't punish us for them.

	Co-creation is not about a performative, relentless faux-happiness that is sometimes referred to as 'toxic positivity'. Rather, it is a method by which we learn to hold our truest desires and our deliberate intentions alongside the things that we cannot control, including the things which may cause us grief or anger.
	Remember, the universe is always working for our highest good. Processing, grieving, healing are all for our highest good.
Myth: *That we must first achieve a level of privilege or success before co-creation will work for us.*	**Truth:** Co-creation is available to us anytime, anywhere, for anyone, always. This is not to imply that it is not easier for some of us to access. When you are living in an unsafe environment, when you are in pain or danger, when the world around you is heartbreaking and unjust, the idea of co-creating the life you desire can feel impossible. Sometimes we must wait for the storm to pass, for our nervous systems to settle, for our basic needs to be met before we can do this work – and that is okay. To be safe, to have our needs met, to feel supported ... these are great gifts, and those of us who are lucky enough to already have these needs met should bring our full aware-ness and deep gratitude to that fact.

The most destructive myths contain a seed of truth; this is why I sometimes refer to them as 'shadow sides' – because often the myth and the truth are two sides of the same coin. So, while it is important to dispel the myth that says we must never think a negative thought, it is also true that the deeper we go into the shadow the quicker we'll get through it and back into the light.

The next few chapters will introduce you to ideas like 'finding neutral' and 'aligning your vibe' which will help you begin to use your mind as a tool, rather than feeling like you are at the mercy of your thoughts.

FYI

Neuroscientist Dr Tara Swart has argued that manifestation works by helping us connect to our thoughts, and that it may even have a positive impact on our neuroplasticity. Neuroplasticity is the brain's ability to change, or to remain *plastic* – that is, moldable and bendy. When we talk about alignment between our beliefs and our desires, we are talking about re-training our brains to adopt new frameworks for understanding ourselves and the world around us. Neuroplasticity involves creating new neural pathways, which we do by practising new habits, adopting new patterns and choosing new systems of belief.

Dr Swart argues that when we allow our brains to really focus on what we want in life, it increases our awareness of opportunities that may be coming our way. Suddenly, we can see possibilities that we might have overlooked – and this in turn helps us to reach our goals and make our dreams come true.[4]

4 Tara Swart, *The Source: The Secrets of the Universe, the Science of the Brain* (HarperCollins, 2019).

Before you move to the next chapter, I invite you to take some time with the information and ideas I've presented to you here about the Law of Attraction, setting deliberate intentions, and discovering your core values and beliefs. Work and play with these ideas. Feel them out, engage with them, and try the journal work I've suggested. And when you feel ready, let's continue.

Part 2

Align Your Vibe: Get ready to co-create!

C o-creation isn't for the lazy or the half-arsed. You need to use your whole arse! Co-creation is a lifestyle. This work will ask you to check your inner monologue and challenge your belief systems. It requires commitment, dedication and sacrifice. It is not always comfortable, it is not always easy. But if you can trust the process, the impact is life-changing. It certainly has been for me.

In Part One, you learned about The Law of Attraction and how we can use our beliefs and core values to set strong intentions; intentions that are matched in frequency by the universe, our partner in co-creation. Another way to describe this is 'aligning your vibe', which is what it sounds like: matching your energy to the energy of what you want to attract.

Soon after I left my violent and abusive relationship, I moved in with my dad. And even though my dad and I have love for each other, it wasn't the best place for me to start to heal. I had no money, I had no job skills, and didn't know where to begin. Because I had been out of work for three years, I didn't even have a resume. I had no idea how to begin putting all the pieces of my life back into place. But I knew I needed a space by myself to feel safe, and that the obstacle to getting this was money.

I wanted to find a place of my own, back near where I once lived with my mum before she died. I felt safe in that area. Closer to her. Although she had been a single mother working two jobs, it was a very affluent neighbourhood; we were the poorest people in it. So, I wasn't sure how I was going to go about finding a place to rent by myself with no job and no funds in such an expensive neighbourhood.

However, by this time, I was starting to learn about manifestation and so I knew that I would need to be feeling a high vibe to attract what I was hoping to call into my life. So I thought: Why not be audacious? You don't have to figure out the *how*! You just have to figure out *what* it is that you want! And so I visualised myself living near the water, feeling safe and secure. I thought about this beautiful walk that my mum and I used to take along Cremorne Point – the crème de la crème of Sydney real estate. I imagined living near the water, somewhere that I would feel safe by myself, and close enough to do that walk I loved so much. I really didn't mind what the place was like. I had grown up in older homes that had been run down, and that felt very comfortable for me – I wasn't precious about that, it wasn't my focus.

And then, this place popped up! It was a studio unit, just one small room. The bathroom was next to a tiny bar fridge, which was next to a tiny little kitchenette. But it was off the Cremorne Point walk. Unbelievable. From there, I could easily stroll down to the path. Sure, the unit was run down, it was probably full of mould, but it was perfect to me. And with divine timing, I got a job babysitting. I was able to put my new job down as proof to the real estate agent that I had work to pay the rent. And I got the studio flat!

I didn't realise it at the time, but all of that visualising and focused attention on the sense of safety that I wanted to feel again, all of that trust – even the fact that I had finally left my dangerous relationship – all of those decisions and actions had put me in a new frame of mind. I had brought my nervous system, my feelings and emotions, my beliefs and values into harmony: I had aligned my vibration. And the universe responded to this vibration and presented me with the most beautiful opportunity – a place where I could heal. I did a lot of healing in that apartment. I remember sobbing, I remember exploring myself, I remember setting boundaries again. It was all so new and my imperfect little space was actually the perfect place to begin.

Now that we have a framework for what co-creation *is*, and how the Law of Attraction and the power of intention allow us to connect with co-creation, it's time to prepare ourselves to take part in this process. Each of the upcoming sections will assist us in refining and mastering this work, but the time to lay the groundwork is now. And the most important thing we can do is to begin the habit of paying close attention to our thoughts. I refer to this as keeping a 'catalogue of thoughts'.

Cataloguing Your Thoughts

I mentioned that the idea that we can 'mess up' our co-creation by having a bad thought or a bad day – or even a bad week – is not only untrue, but also causes a lot of confusion and pain for people who misunderstand this work as a result. But that isn't to say that our thoughts don't matter. Our thoughts *are* important.

We must begin to discern between obsessive negative thought-looping – the cycle of thoughts that make us cynical and holds us in a pattern of negative emotion – and the very appropriate negative emotions we may feel in life, such as the grief we feel when we lose a loved one. The more we practise understanding the difference, the more we can identify which emotions and thoughts actually require our attention, and which are simply unhelpful thought-habits we have formed over time.

The best way to do this is by keeping a list. I love a list! Make a deliberate effort to notice the thoughts that take over your mind throughout your day and write them down. If you can notice what emotions and feelings those thoughts produce, even better.

For example, when I first started to write down my thoughts it looked a lot like this:

I'm running late for work. I'm such an idiot. Why did I stay up late watching TV? I just love to finish something once I've started it. But I hate waking up tired; I'm so mad at myself. I obviously have no self-respect. My presentation is today and I am SO tired. God, I don't deserve this job. I'm so dumb. I ruin everything. And I'm so hungry, but I didn't pack lunch for work. I made that amazing pasta last night and forgot to bring the leftovers. I'm so organised at work, but I can't even remember to pack lunch? I'm going to order something. Ugh, but I shouldn't! I'm really trying to save. Why can't I manage my life like a normal person? Okay, I will order sushi and then not let myself spend any more money. I am actually a really good saver when I'm focused.

You can probably see that there are a LOT of negative thoughts in there. But there are also a few positive ones: I admitted that I am good at finishing things once I start them, which shows dedication – even if it's only to binge-watching a TV show. And I acknowledge that the meal I made was amazing, so I am proud of my skills in the kitchen. I have recognised that I'm usually very organised in my work life, but that there's some room for improvement on the home front. And I also identify that I am pretty good at saving, even if I sometimes have a few slip-ups.

As you start to see the quality of your own thoughts, pay special attention to what I refer to as negative self-talk or intrusive thoughts. We can be very mean to ourselves in the privacy of our mind. So it's understandable that many of us have a habit of reinforcing the negative thoughts about ourselves, the self-doubt and the imposter syndrome that creeps in when we try something new. Write these thoughts down, too, but then ask yourself: *Would I speak to a friend like this? Would I say this to my child or my partner? Would I allow someone else to speak to me this way?* The answer is no. But what can we do with these intrusive negative thoughts so that they have less of an impact on our energy? The best thing we can do is to acknowledge them, and respond as if we were the kindest, most loving versions of ourselves, soothing this berating voice inside of us. We want to catch those thoughts before they spiral. Love them and then move on. Once we have done that we can begin the process of replacing this negative and detrimental self-talk with positive, encouraging words and affirmation.

As you start to check your thoughts and become more deliberate about which thoughts you consciously choose to focus on and which ones you let go of, you will begin to clear the way to really tune into what you desire, and, more importantly, *why* you desire it. That's one of the reasons people are attracted to the idea of manifestation; the idea that you are able to turn your desires into reality. The following sections will give you the tools you need to co-create successfully, but it's important to begin with firm foundations.

FYI

Did you know that there is a science to habit forming? Because habit forming is a type of learning, and we all learn in different ways, it's important to know that this is not a one-size-fits-all kind of thing. We all bring different factors to the habit-forming table which determine how long it might take us to create new ones. But there are some useful generalisations we can take away from science.

One of the most widely-cited studies on habit forming was conducted by Dr Phillippa Lally, a senior lecturer in psychology and the co-director of the Habit Application and Theory group at the University of Surrey in England. She looked at how the participants in her study incorporated three new daily habits into their lives: eating a piece of fruit, drinking a bottle of water and running for fifteen minutes. Lally's study found that the number of days it took for participants to incorporate these new habits into their lives ranged between 18 and 254, with an average of 66 days. The secret? Repetition and consistency.[5] This is why I talk about co-creation as a lifestyle, and not just something we dip in and out of. Because the more we incorporate co-creation into our lives, the more we practise the habits and behaviours that set us up for success, the sooner these habits become a part of who we are.

Lally's study also revealed another key factor in forming habits, which she referred to as 'context'. When the habit was performed in the same context – for example, at the same time every day, or

---

5   Phillippa Lally *et al*, 'How Are Habits Formed?: Modelling habit formation in the real world' *European Journal of Social Psychology* 40(6) (October 2020).

in the same place – it was much easier for participants to maintain.[6] So, when you're thinking about forming new habits to support your co-creation practice, consider when, where and how. Try setting a time to catalogue your thoughts each day, or make a decision to journal for five minutes every time you sit down at your desk or as soon as you wake up in the morning.

Attaining Neutral

An important part of the co-creation process is what I like to call attaining a state of 'neutral'. People often ask, 'Do I need to heal all of my trauma, fix every issue in my life and fully calm the chaos of my personal situation before I can start?' Absolutely not. The only thing you need to do is find neutral.

Neutral is exactly what it sounds like. You are not in a fight, flight, fawn or freeze state. Your nervous system is in neutral. So how do you do this if you are in a seriously chaotic or scary situation? You will need to remove yourself from any environment that makes you feel physically unsafe. This may be the time you need to put down this book and seek help from a friend or family member, or even a therapist.

We need to be in a neutral state to begin. If you are in a safe environment but your mind is chaos, this we can work with. As long as your physical state is not in danger you have the ability to get to neutral.

Neutral feels like empty space. It feels like openness and curiosity. It is a state of balanced emotions (this doesn't mean

---

6   Phillippa Lally et al, 'How Are Habits Formed?: Modelling habit formation in the real world' *European Journal of Social Psychology* 40(6) (October 2020).

you won't experience *uncomfortable* emotions, it just means that there is room for both the light and the shade). It is neither a state of super heightened excitement, nor deep anxiety or depression. It means that you could be feeling a low simmer of excitement, or a low simmer of anxiety, but no one emotion is dominant.

Neutral can feel like an average day where nothing much happens, where the monotony and routine of your day-to-day life is just kind of cruising along. You may carry grief and sorrow for the losses you've experienced, you may still feel activated when you think about certain disappointments, but you have made it to the other side.

Neutral is when the intensity of the immediacy of the pain that life brings with it has dissipated enough to let you catch your breath. To use my own example, I found neutral after I had grieved and begun to process a lot of that intense trauma I'd experienced over the death of my mother and my abusive relationship. I wasn't completely healed, I wasn't perfect, I still wasn't feeling great. But it was a place where my basic needs were met and I was safe. My nervous system wasn't in fight-or-flight mode, and I was able to be calm and focused enough to make a choice: the choice to work with the universe to create the life that I wanted and deserved.

This is neutral. It is important to acknowledge that feeling neutral is one of the greatest privileges we can have in life. If you have the ability to have your most basic needs met – safety, shelter, food, rest – then you are able to focus your attention in ways that are far more difficult when we are in survival mode with a nervous system in a fight-or-flight state. I know what it's like to be in fight-or-flight. And it is possible to find your way back to neutral, but it may require that you tend to your most immediate needs first. Pause, ask for help and find neutral.

But, if you've picked up this book and are reading these words right now, chances are you're already in neutral. Which means: you're ready. You're prepared. You have everything you need to keep going down this path.

FYI

American sociologist Abraham Maslow theorised that our most basic needs must be met before we can focus on our higher selves. In Maslow's hierarchy of needs, our most basic needs support all others: food, water, sleep and breathing form the base of his pyramid. Next is our safety: our homes, our physical bodies, our families and our jobs must be relatively safe and stable before we can truly focus on what's at the top of the pyramid: love and belonging, self-esteem and self-actualisation (which is all about creativity, morality and becoming our best selves).

Finding neutral before we begin to co-create isn't about achieving perfection or solving every problem – it's about meeting the minimum requirements that will allow us the time and space to focus our energy and cultivate the right state of mind to be able to manifest those things we desire.

Cultivating a Mindset of Abundance

Do you *feel* rich, healthy and happy? Do you *feel* like incredible people and opportunities are drawn to you? Do you *feel* that you are truly living your best life – an abundant, joyful life that is giving you all that you want and need?

If yes, amazing! You can put this book down as you are already a master at co-creation. But if you're not quite there yet, like most of us, this mindset of abundance feels very foreign and out of reach, especially if our current reality is anchored in the opposite mindset: scarcity.

Unless we were born and raised by master co-creators, the majority of us need to make a conscious choice to learn and develop an abundant mindset. My favourite thing about this mindset is how it supports our journey with co-creation and also *feels* really good at the same time.

An abundant mindset is a prosperous mindset. It's glass-half-full, it's optimistic and it's what some like to call 'lucky girl syndrome'. Feeling abundant can mean different things to different people. Personally, it means knowing that all my needs are met, that the world has many incredible people, opportunities and experiences waiting for me. It means believing that life is full of possibility. It means trusting that there is always enough for me and for others. Think about it: What is the opposite of abundance? Scarcity. So, we are cultivating a mindset that directs us away from a sense of scarcity or impossibility, towards a sense of abundance and possibility – even probability.

As we now know, our belief systems have been instilled in us since childhood, and they can be challenging to change. When we are taught that we are given the cards we are dealt and that's just the way it is, it can feel difficult to change that mindset. It can feel confronting to challenge these belief systems. But, once we do, there's so much freedom and power in understanding that we don't need anyone else's permission to create the life we want. You are the creator of your life, and it is vital to cultivate a mindset that accepts this truth: an abundant mindset.

We create this mindset by recognising the things we already have in our lives and realising that more will follow. Take note of what you have: it can be as simple as a roof over your head, good food and clean water, people you care about. You have this book, and you are reading these words on a page. These are all things you have in your life right now – and they are just the start of what is to come. A mindset of abundance is all about taking notice of what you already have, remembering that like attracts like, and trusting that more will follow.

Instead of looking at your bank balance and worrying that you aren't saving as much as you would like, look at it and acknowledge what's there, and trust that more will come. Always focus on the end result: really feel it. Instead of worrying about what would happen if you were to lose your job, remember that you got the job in the first place – you were the *best* candidate, and even if you did lose your job, you already have all the skills you need to attract a new role; and with a mindset of abundance working for you, it will be a better one.

I remember sitting in my little studio and feeling like the richest girl in the world, I was free. Being in that space created a true mindset of abundance that anything and everything was possible.

And, as you will come to realise, this feeling of abundance is matched by the universe. The Law of Attraction. Like attracts like. Marry that feeling with whatever you are calling in and you will be matched with something else that makes you feel ever more abundant.

Creating an Attitude of Gratitude

You have probably noticed that the principles of co-creation or manifestation are like a tightly woven tapestry. Gratitude, abundance, values, beliefs, intention . . . these ideas don't exist alone nor are they a step-by-step kind of thing. They all exist in relationship with each other and sometimes they all operate together in service of co-creation. Gratitude is paramount to the process, and now it's time to go deeper on this principle.

We talked about the power of gratitude when we discussed the Law of Attraction. But gratitude is something we will come back to again and again. The more we ruminate on gratitude, the more we deepen our understanding and awareness of what it really means, what it feels like, what it offers to the universe. And the more we practise, the better we will become at maintaining a state of gratitude, until it becomes our default setting: our autopilot. Even when shit hits the fan, we will be able to find something to be grateful for amongst the chaos of the moment.

Gratitude is a form of deep acknowledgement and appreciation. While we can express our gratitude in words, true gratitude is a feeling. The more grateful we *feel* for what we have, the more good things we attract into our lives.

For example, you may want to co-create a new place to live – just like I did when I began searching for my little flat, my space to heal. But can you also tap into the gratitude for the home you have now? Can you focus on your cosy bed with your comfy favourite pillow? Access to a hot shower and clean towels to dry off with? The fact that you have an oven you can prepare meals in? Maybe it's the view out of your bedroom window, or the tree in your front yard. Obviously, there are things you don't like about your current home, which is why you are co-creating a new one. But if you can tune into what you already have, what is present in your life, and truly feel the gratitude . . . you know what happens: the Law of Attraction will give you more of what you are focused on and grateful for. Gratitude is a way of saying, 'This *feels* good, I *like* this.' It's a signal to the universe to do its part to send you more things that also feel good and that you will also be grateful for. It's a cycle: a powerful manifestation cycle.

I love gratitude lists. I keep them in a gratitude journal, which I like to re-read over the years so that I can acknowledge all the things I've been blessed with and feel all of that gratitude all over again. As you continue to master co-creation, you will find that you create your own bespoke rituals and habits that help to bring you into that sweet spot of alignment. You will create your own perfect way that works for you. But I'll give you a glimpse of what my gratitude lists look like, and I hope they inspire you to see that there is nothing too small, too insignificant or even *seemingly* insignificant to be grateful for. I am thinking about how grateful I am for my ability to write these words to you *as I write them.* I am grateful that you – *you* specifically – are reading these words right at this exact moment.

ZOE'S GRATITUDE LIST

Today, I am grateful . . .
- That I was educated in a system that taught me to read and write and be able to access the world of ideas that live inside books.

- For books. And paper and pens and ink and all of the innovation and creativity that went into inventing them.
- For the tea that I am drinking right now, those tea leaves, the earth they grew from, and the entire process that got this tea into my hands. A miracle.
- That I have access to a piece of fresh fruit in my refrigerator that I can cut up and share with my children – how fortunate we are to access nourishing foods for our bodies.

I could go on and on and on . . .

Try writing your own gratitude list. Start with the little things and gradually work towards those bigger things that make life worth living: the things that you have achieved, the people you love, your purpose. There is so much to be grateful for, but often we are get used to taking it all for granted. Once you shift your lens into gratitude you will see that little miracles are everywhere, and as you tap into this feeling more and more miracles will meet you.

The last thing that really helps us drop into gratitude and fast track our manifestation may also be the thing we find the most challenging. This is what I like to call 'feeling the end result'. It's all about living, acting, moving, speaking as if this manifestation has already arrived and it is yours. It's feeling your way into gratitude for the things you want before they have arrived. If you are calling in romantic love, I want you to try to *feel* what having received that love is like. As if you have already met your life partner. Is there warmth filling your chest, is there safety in your heart? Feel gratitude for finding this person.

When I married my husband, we wrote our own vows. And I told him: 'I'm grateful to God that we met at the very point in life where we could accept this life-changing love, thank you for loving me.' The best part – I had already felt this exact same feeling of gratitude long ago, before I even met Benji. I had visualised meeting the man I would spend the rest of my life with, and then I allowed myself to feel grateful for him. So, when it came time to say my wedding vows, it was a serious case of déjà vu. The universe doesn't know the difference between feeling thankful for what we already have and being thankful for what we want – it only knows that we are thankful. So it sends us more things to be thankful for.

We've explored how to understand where our desires come from and how to connect to the feelings they create. This aligns those desires with our core values. And now it's time to be grateful for that new apartment even when you're still living in your current one; be grateful for the amazing new job opportunity you're going to get while you're still working in your current position. And I know from experience, it might feel weird at first, like a form of self-delusion – but as the kids say, 'Delulu is the solulu!'

Try it, you have nothing to lose. Keep trying, and soon you will see how the universe responds to this practice – and you'll have all the evidence you need that it works.

FYI

There is growing scientific evidence that gratitude has a positive impact on our minds and our bodies. A 2023 study showed that people who consciously practice gratitude tended to have better outcomes when it came to stress, sleep and even mental health.[7] Another study showed that daily gratitude journalling may even help reduce or alleviate chronic pain.[8] In a 2017 study from Korea, researchers scanned participants' brains and measured their heart rates while they engaged in a 'gratitude intervention', and were able to show that a state of gratitude can impact our nervous system by slowing our heart rate and encouraging relaxation. The scientists concluded that practicing gratitude has a positive impact on 'mental well-being as a means of improving not only emotion regulation, but also self-motivation'.[9]

Retraining our minds to look for the things we are grateful for, rather than the things we are upset about, fearful of, or triggered by, can create new neural pathways that have a monumental impact on how we experience the world. And there's so much to be grateful for!

Clarifying Your Desires and Goals

Sometimes, we don't know what it is we really want or need in our lives. And at other times, we might know what we want, but struggle to understand *why* we want it. Starting with clarity

---

7   Melissa Makhoul and E. J. Bartley, 'Exploring the relationship between gratitude and depression among older adults with chronic low back pain: A sequential mediation analysis' *Frontiers in Pain Research* 4 (5 May 2023).

8   Shelley Condon, Brian Cox and Patricia Parmelee, 'Cultivating an Attitude of Gratitude: A Brief Gratitude Invervention for Older Adults with Chronic Pain' *Innovation in Aging* 7 (21 December 2023).

9   Sunghyon Kyeong *et al*, 'Effects of gratitude medidation on neural network functional connectivity and brain–heart coupling' *Scientific Reports* 7 (11 July 2017).

around your wants is an essential part of co-creation; it gives you direction, focus and motivation, and it provides the universe with clarity about what you are ready to receive.

Once you've found neutral and have shifted your mindset towards abundance and gratitude, it's time to bring what you want into focus by following these steps:

Step One: Identify your manifestation

Write down your desires and goals. If you have a long list, choose one to work with now, so that you can give this manifestation your full focus. If there is not a specific thing that you can identify, focus instead on the feeling that you want to manifest. Do you want more happiness, joy, creativity, purpose, love or connection? You can absolutely focus your co-creation around a feeling as much as you can around a thing.

Step Two: Feel it out

Sit with this manifestation for a few minutes. What feelings does it produce? What sensations do you feel in your body? Tune in to your gut. Does it feel restless and nervous or calm and steady? Ask yourself: Does this desire serve me in the most positive, healthy, authentic way possible? If you feel that true inner *yes*... this is where you want to be! But if you sense that perhaps this desire isn't really connected to your core values, it's worth investigating that feeling. And that takes us to the next step.

Step Three: Find your *why*

Check in with your *why*. Why do you want what you want? Be as honest with yourself as you can, with no judgement. Sometimes we believe, for example, that what our parents, partner, friends or colleagues want for us is what we want for ourselves, and it's not until we really question our manifestations that we discover that it isn't.

We all have egos, it's part of the human condition. However, when our manifestations are purely ego-driven they don't always manifest in the way we'd like them to. On the other hand, desires that come from a place of truth – desires that align with our core values – operate on a much higher frequency and the co-creation process flows more freely, on a higher vibration.

To determine the true origins of your desire, ask yourself a few simple questions:

- Are you trying to please or impress someone; your parents or peers or partner?
- Are you trying to prove something to someone?
- Are you hoping that achieving this desire, whatever it is, will heal an unresolved trauma or problem?
- Are you approaching manifestation as a quick fix solution; are you using it to avoid something more profound or important?

If you answered yes to any of the above, it's a sign that this is an ego-driven want. This isn't bad or wrong – we've all sought external validation in our lives. But it is an opportunity to look a little deeper and to try to avoid the blocks that ego can create. When we reflect on our motivations and make sure that our goals align with our truest self, what we are manifesting becomes anchored in deep trust that this is for our greater good, the highest version of ourselves. Noticing when our ego is driving our manifestations doesn't mean we necessarily have to give up on them. Rather, it means that we move on to step four.

Step Four: Align your manifestation

Now it's time to align your manifestation with your core values. Maybe what you're visualising is a new job or promotion. And when you were finding your why, you recognised that part of the reason you want this job is that you believe other people might find you more impressive: that other people will realise how wrong they've been. These are very human, normal things to feel, but manifestations that are driven by negative emotions like feelings of worthlessness and self-doubt can create blocks – these manifestations don't flow easily because they don't serve our highest good. Instead of bringing in what we *want*, they can end up creating more of what we're trying to escape: a sense of unease, being misunderstood, or frustrations with other people. Because, as we've learned, the Law of Attraction gives us more of what we're focusing on.

Understanding this, how can you re-imagine what this new job means to you? It's all about where that want is coming from. Think of yourself as a fish struggling to survive in a polluted lake. In that unhealthy environment, there's no way for the fish to thrive. But in a clear, healthy stream, it's a completely different story. The fish was never a failure, it just needed to be in the right environment. In the same way, your manifestations can only thrive in a pure and healthy place – they won't stand a chance in a toxic wasteland driven by ego or what other people think.

Think back to your core values. Consider re-reading the list that you wrote in your journal. Can you identify the relationship between your core values and your longing for a new job or promotion? Can you connect this manifestation to a feeling that works on a higher frequency? Can you feel the pride and sense of achievement you will experience when you get that new position?

If one of your core values is creativity, you could focus on all the ways this new job would allow you to be more creative. If you value helping others, you might focus on how you will be able to inspire your team.

The big, new job can be yours. The universe will co-create this big, new job with you. And when it is connected to the frequency of healthy and positive intention, the world's your oyster.

Now you're clear on your goal or desire and you have aligned it with your core values, you're in the perfect place to begin to co-create it. There's just one more piece that can really help bring your manifestations to life, and that is finding your 'riisers'.

Finding Your Riisers

As human beings, we are wired to pay close attention to each other. We are a community-based species, and we need each other to survive. It's natural to notice when someone has more than you. Maybe they have the job you wish you had, or a partner you long for. Sometimes this can make us feel envy, anger or even a sense of injustice, and we can start to create stories that the people who have what we want are not on our team, that they are our competition. But what if those people who have the things we want are actually our greatest inspiration to co-create? I call them 'riisers'. Use that initial feeling of envy to identify who your riisers are and take the opportunity to learn from them. Don't avoid them – actively seek them out.

As we get clear on what we want to manifest, we become aware of people who already have those things that we want. And, as I have mentioned, this can make us feel envious. This is a real, human emotion. The trick is to learn to see envy as an opportunity to strengthen your ability to co-create. If you get caught up and find yourself in an envy loop, it will create a major block to the co-creation process. This is the Law of Attraction: envy is connected to lack and scarcity, to not having something that you desperately want – and if you focus on lack and scarcity, the universe will give you more . . .? Lack and scarcity!

But there is a super effective way to stop the envy loop. This is a process I call 'finding your riisers'.

Riisers are people that have come from where you are and have what you want. When we change our perspective from envy to appreciation, we can see these people as inspiration. Because riisers are evidence that what you desire is attainable and achievable. Think of them as your co-creation guides who can help you shift frustration into motivation.

So, where can we find our riisers? For one thing, it's important to focus on real people and not fictional characters, as we are seeking evidence that our manifestations can be achieved in the real world. When you find people who have gained or achieved what you are seeking to create – congratulate them. Ask them questions, support their work, acknowledge the co-creation that went into the life they are living and find out how they did it. Focus on the positive sensations of seeing your riiser thrive, learn from them, and then feel into it. Act as if what you're calling in is already yours, and the universe will start to send you opportunities, people and circumstances that bring more of this feeling.

A great thing about riisers is that they tend to come into your life just when you need them the most. Let me tell you a little story about finding my riisers, and how they helped me in my co-creation practice.

Ariise

Growing up, I had always wanted to be an actor – I dreamed of performing in the theatre and in movies. I started drama classes at nine years old and went on to study at Actors Centre Australia for three years. I longed to be a film star. I auditioned for every single Aussie drama and never got the break I needed. I performed in co-op theatre and short films as well as many, many TV commercials.

A year after I had left my abusive relationship and had moved into my tiny flat alone, busy with nannying work to pay the rent, I started to teach acting part-time at primary schools (fun fact: it was the school my son goes to now. Coincidence? I think not). I loved it – it felt like I was returning to my passion. I was rebuilding my confidence. And it was at this time that I started to look outside myself for riisers: those people who have come from similar beginnings as we have, but who are currently living exceptional lives, having great experiences, and creating the kind of work opportunities and meaningful relationships that we aspire to.

I remember living in this tiny place and having a strong desire to stop babysitting and go back to the world of performing, so I started looking around to see who was hosting TV shows and doing all the big TV ads, and who had been signed by the best agents. It turned out that a lot of them were my peers, friends or people that I had gone to drama school with. These people who were having great success were just like me. Did I have twinges of envy? Of course! I'm a human being. But I quickly moved past those lower vibration emotions and really examined what I was observing. That's when I had a light bulb moment. I thought to myself: if they're able to make money from their talent and skills, I can do the same. In fact, I had a lot of the same talents and skills as they did. As soon as I chose to see them as sources of inspiration instead of sources of envy or shame, there was a switch, the focus was suddenly on my own ambition and passion because I'd left behind those negative thoughts.

I remember doing some calculations. My rent at that time was $300 per week. If I could find a TV presenting job for $500 a week then I could give up babysitting. I found a call-out for a TV show host on a really budget audition site. I researched the producers of the show and googled who the old hosts were. I found out as much as I possibly could about them. I learnt that one of the previous hosts was a woman named Lizzy Lovette and I immediately started researching her career. She was bubbly and smiley and had appeared in a handful of shows I recognised. I was inspired by her career, as it didn't feel out of reach for me. I looked around and noticed that close friends of mine from drama school were getting great jobs in the industry: my school buddy Daniel Henshall was the star of a huge new Aussie film called *Snowtown*, while another bestie was in a stage production at Belvoir Street Theatre performing as a lead in *Steel Magnolias*. I had found my riisers!

At the same time, I began to tell myself that, like my riisers, I had talent too. And I had proof, we were all at the same school together, weren't we? I could do this hosting job. I began to stretch the boundaries of my self-worth, to believe that I deserved this job, and that it was mine for the taking.

But, as I would learn later, co-creation requires effort. We must take aligned action (more on this in the next chapter) to work towards what we want. So, I enrolled in presenting classes, continued my research and looked for an agent. I believed – in fact, I *knew* – that I was worthy of this opportunity. It was a teeny tiny show, a drop in the giant ocean of television, which felt like a perfect place to start: it felt achievable and realistic. I started to visualise myself living the end result and began to believe it was my job before it was mine at all.

When I showed up for the audition I was so prepared and inspired by my riisers that I felt confident and ready to face anything. And then, the essential part: I let it all go, and I was just myself. I workshopped alongside a few male co-hosts, and I remember walking out of the audition and calling my then boyfriend Benji (who is now my sexy husband and the father of my children) and telling him: 'That job is mine!' (It definitely wasn't yet.) 'I can really feel it. It's mine. It is.'

Did I find myself getting a little bit anxious while I waited to hear their decision? A little worried? Of course! But every time I found myself slipping into a mindset of scarcity, I thought about my friends who were having success, not only the actors I mentioned above, but all of the people in my life who were achieving big goals and living their dreams.

Motivational speaker Jim Rohn famously said that we are the average of the five people we spend the most time with. Riisers are an amazing way of upping your average! Even though my riisers weren't in my immediate circle, I realised the impact of being around positive, successful, ambitious friends. The people I was drawn to were aligning me and keeping me accountable. I'd surrounded myself with riisers in all categories. My career riisers became a source of inspiration, keeping me focused, reminding me that these opportunities are offered to people every day.

A week later, the producers called me and told me that I got the job. And although eventually I would change course again – our manifestations and dreams change and evolve – it was the beginning of a career which led me to this moment, right now: writing you this book that I know will change your life. We have now learned how we can align our vibration with the universe and prepare ourselves to co-create anything we want. In the next section, we'll look at the tools we will need to make it all happen.

Part 3

Your Co-creation Toolkit

As we evolve to this new way of being, it can be helpful to pause and take note of what we have learned so far, and to revisit the principles that will help us to move forward with clarity. You have taken the time to understand what co-creation is and how it uses the Law of Attraction to manifest what you want. You have been thinking deeply about your core values, your beliefs and your intentions. You have learned how to catalogue your thoughts, what it means to find neutral, and how to cultivate a mindset of abundance and gratitude. You've even begun to search for inspiration in the form of riisers – the people who have proven that what you want is possible. Look at all you have achieved! You are in the perfect place to take the next step.

In this section, we're going to learn all the tools that we need to co-create the life we deserve. These are tools I've discovered and refined over time, the techniques that have helped me create my own practice. From how to meditate, visualise and direct your precious attention to where it belongs, to using your words wisely and discovering simple ways to develop routines and rituals that will help you manifest what you *really* want.

Use Your Words

We have paid a lot of attention to cultivating an awareness of how we feel, of how we think, of what we believe. But there is another factor to consider as you become master co-creators: what we say.

The easiest way to form new beliefs that align with our higher selves is through language. This expedites our alignment with the universe. Words are powerful. There is a reason that most of the world's religions and spiritual movements include mantras, prayers, hymns and sacred texts. How we speak impacts our vibration and strengthens our belief systems – for good or bad.

It takes time to trust that the universe wants the best for us, and that it's always working for our greater good. We need to help this process by changing the way we talk to ourselves, whether in our minds or out loud. It's time to challenge the nasty things we say or think (perhaps without even knowing it), to reframe our thoughts, to get audacious with what we want to co-create, and, of course, to deeply trust that the universe has our back.

This means we must choose our words wisely. Speak with integrity. And when we are manifesting, we must speak as if what we want is already ours. The universe responds to the readiness it is receiving from your words, feelings and vibration, and language plays a big role in this. For example, instead of saying, 'I want an abundance of money to take my family on a holiday,' try saying, 'I *have* the means and the abundance to take my family on a holiday!' And this is the important part – really *feel* what that would be like. Believe your words. Let that sense of excitement and financial ease and joy and readiness fill you up. Talk about all the things you're most excited about on your holiday: having a piña colada, jumping in the ocean on a perfect sunny day, the water feeling just right. Talk about flopping onto the bed exhausted post-shower after being in the sand and salt water all day. Bliss! Speak as if you are already living with what you want and desire.

This could feel a little silly at the start. But the truth is that some of the most successful people in the world use this method – and a little bit of silliness is a small price to pay. From Oprah to Drake and even Travis Kelce manifesting his relationship with Taylor Swift, many successful people use the techniques of manifestation to help turn their dreams into reality. And when you try this yourself, you will start to see your life transform.

However, it's important to remember that this can also be a private practice that you may choose to keep secret. It's intimate and vulnerable and it's yours. You don't have to share it with anyone else if you don't want to. But manifestors recognise each other. We just don't always say it out loud. It's like being in a secret society: the ones that get it, *get it*.

But even within this process, it's important to acknowledge when it's appropriate to share our struggles or pain. Perhaps you are in physical pain. Perhaps you are struggling financially. Perhaps you are deeply worried about the state of the world, or just feeling particularly exhausted. These are all valid human experiences and emotions, and there are times when it is perfectly appropriate to share this information with other people. When we keep our pain to ourselves, it can have a very detrimental effect on our mental health. Yet, there is a difference between sharing our pain with the intention of seeking a solution, and complaining for complaining's sake, catastrophising and dramatising out of habit or because we want an audience for our suffering.

It can be helpful to notice when we have become a little too obsessed with sharing our pain and fear, our frustrations and challenges. Focusing too much on these things can have a paralysing effect and can stop us from taking action. Sometimes this feeling of paralysis is referred to as 'learned helplessness' or 'learned suffering'. This occurs when we have experienced challenging moments and have recieved attention or support. In those moments, we may accidentally stumble into a sense of power in being the victim or the sufferer. It becomes more comfortable to talk about our suffering than to do something to help change it.

In this state, we see everything through the lens of our suffering. When we have conversations with people, we may find that we are always sharing our problems. And we do this knowing that the conversation isn't solution or healing focused, it is aimed at getting other people to acknowledge our suffering. The ego craves this. We all fall into this pattern from time to time, because we all have egos that desperately need validation. And if we are unhappy, or things in our life feel unfair, we want someone to confirm that we are right in our feelings.

In order to break the cycle, we have to be conscious of the words that come out of our mouths and how dwelling on negative experiences in our conversations with others can trap us in feelings of victimhood. Check in, is this you? Is this who you want to be? Language is a powerful tool and one that needs respect and practice: it creates our future. The language we use keeps us in alignment with the universe or higher power.

The comedian Craig Ferguson is often credited with popularising the three questions we should ask ourselves before we speak:

1. Does this need to be said?
2. Does this need to be said by me?
3. Does this need to be said by me, right now?

It's a powerful way to learn to be more deliberate with our words, and to recognise their power. The Buddha also taught the principle of being deliberate and mindful about our language. He referred to it as 'Right Speech' and divided it into four categories:

1. Abstaining from false speech.
2. Abstaining from slanderous speech.
3. Abstaining from harsh speech.
4. Abstaining from idle chatter.

This is encouraging us to be truthful, to avoid talking shit and gossiping and to be kind and deliberate with our words. These guidelines teach us how to be mindful of our language and its effects on us personally as well as on the world around us.

Like everything, this is a practice. It's something we get better at the more we do it. It's okay to take baby steps. Personally, I am an evidence gatherer. I like to test these principles to see how they really show up in my life. Try challenging yourself to make it through just one day where you are exceptionally mindful of every word you speak. Make note of how you feel when you move through the world this way. Did you feel more positive and purposeful? Did it feel good enough to try it for one more day? And another? Be gentle with yourself, take it one day at a time, and eventually those days will string together and become your lifestyle – and that is what this work is all about.

Let me share with you a little secret: the first thing that I do when I wake up in the morning – before anything else – is say a declaration or affirmation. It could be: 'Today is going to be a great day.' Or: 'Opportunities find me.' I've taught my children this habit, too. Imagine learning this when you are young, and those neural pathways are still being developed! Our words are so powerful – we just need to learn how to use them.

Affirmations

A powerful way that we can use our words is with the fine art of affirmation. To affirm is to acknowledge the reality and presence of something or someone. It is also to acknowledge the truth and essence of something or someone. This has been referred to as 'positive thinking' or 'words of encouragement' – and essentially, that is what affirmations are. They are words that contain the ability to shift your perspective, your mood and even your beliefs.

Affirmations are statements we say aloud or in our minds that bring positive change. They can shift beliefs – I often call them declarations because they are positive statements that we are declaring to the universe. Affirmations work their best when they're repeated often. The benefit of repeating an affirmation – especially when it is mixed with emotion – is that it helps to form a neural pathway that in turn becomes a belief. This is a huge part of shifting the way we see the world and ourselves; it helps us feel *deserving* of the things we are co-creating. Feeling deserving is essential. It truly is the key.

To find the affirmation that you need, scan through your mind and body, your current circumstances and any emotional or practical blocks, and see what is lacking or what you may need. It could start as something like: 'I don't feel smart enough.' Changing that into a positive affirmation sounds like: 'I have all the wisdom inside me; everything I need to learn comes effortlessly and easily. I am infinitely intelligent.' Why not try out some of my favourite affirmations in the box below?

Affirmations

I let go, and let the universe reveal what it is I need to know and when I need to know it.

I trust the timing of my life, everything works out for me.

Money flows easily and effortlessly to me.

I am abundant and all my needs are met.

Life is working for me, never against me.

Opportunities find me, I am in the right place at the right time.

I am looked after, safe and divinely protected.

I matter, I make a difference in my community, my family and the world.

I am on the right path, constantly supported by my higher power.

I am enough, I am loved.

I love myself.

♥

Precious Attention

Your attention is a very precious thing. And it's in hot demand. Tech companies, brands and the media are always going to incredible lengths to snatch it from us. They know that it is not only a precious commodity but also that it is a finite one, and figuring out how to capture and control it is a lucrative business. But to be looking *at* something is to be looking *away* from something else.

Every school report card I received since I was five said that I was 'easily distracted', so I understand this at a deep level. There is so much constantly coming at us that it's easy to feel like we don't have control over where our attention goes – our eyes (and our minds) are simply pulled in whatever direction the loudest, brightest screen may be, and sometimes everywhere at once. Since when did we become constantly available? Since when did it become okay for anyone who needs or wants something from us to demand it immediately, and expect us to give them our precious attention?

Our attention is invaluable, and we are in charge of who and what we give it to. It's important to guard our attention, and make sure we have enough of it to give to the things that are important to us – especially to our co-creation practice.

Where your attention goes is fundamental to your mental and emotional wellbeing and it has profound effects on your mindset and co-creation abilities. It always comes back to this major principle: what we give our attention and focus to, we get more of. A helpful reminder is the saying, 'Where attention goes, energy flows.' When we focus on things that make us feel good, joyful, fun and in flow and ease, we start to experience more joy, fun, flow and ease. Alternatively, if we choose to focus on the negative aspects of our lives then we are likely to experience more of the same.

Imagine that you wake up every day with a tea pot full of attention. Everything you choose to focus on throughout the day takes a teacup, or maybe a mug's worth of attention from that tea pot. Instead of mindlessly pouring out our attention, it's important to think about how we can make it to the end of the day with some attention left in our teapot just for us, to focus on our wellbeing and self-care.

Now that we have learned to create a catalogue of our thoughts, and to write down our core values and beliefs, it's important to see what takes up our focus and attention. What TV shows are you watching? What podcasts are you listening to? What are you reading? What are you learning? What kind of conversations are you having with other people and what kind of company do you keep?

Things that don't deserve our precious attention

- *ANTI-SOCIAL MEDIA*: Social media is particularly tricky. It can be important for our work, a source of inspiration or even a place to find our riisers, but it can also make us feel terrible and drown us in a sea of negative content or comparison. Every so often I like to do an edit of who I follow on social media, unfollowing anything that doesn't feel good, and only following those things that contribute high, happy and positive vibes. Any media – including social media – that makes you feel less than does not deserve your precious attention. If something that you are consuming makes you compare yourself negatively to others, or brings your high vibe down, it's time to cut it out of your life. But it's important to note that this is a very personal thing, and there's no strictly 'good' or 'bad' media. If following a fitness blogger makes you feel motivated and excited about your gym goals – that's great! Keep following. But if watching their content leaves you feeling awful, ashamed and less than, then it's time to unfollow (although it's worth remembering that we do have the ability to turn envy into awe!). If listening to a true crime podcast entertains and educates you and you feel a sense of justice and satisfaction when listening – that's completely fine, you do you. But if that podcast keeps you up at night with worries about murders and kidnappings, you might want to rethink whether it really deserves your precious attention.

- *NEGATIVITY*: Going out and socialising with friends, family and co-workers is really important. But we have all experienced the way negative patterns can evolve in certain relationship dynamics. Perhaps your co-workers always complain about their jobs whenever you catch up for a Friday night drink after work? Or maybe you have a friend who constantly complains about their partner, but never makes any attempt to work on their relationship issues? You don't need to stop socialising with your co-workers or your friend, but it's crucial to protect your precious attention. Ask yourself: do these people expect you to join in as some type of bonding? Misery loves company. And yes, we have all bonded over shitty bosses or partners and that can be validating at times, but when it becomes the main flavour of your relationship remember that you have the power to shift that. This could mean redirecting the conversation, or finding a way to reframe their perspective. Maybe it's time to be honest and acknowledge that you have contributed to the negativity because it made you feel a sense of belonging? Tell your friend or coworkers that you've noticed you've got stuck in a cycle, and you have some ideas on how to shift the conversation. Need an idea? Use this book as a talking point and discuss all the things you've learned so far as a way to change the vibe of the relationship to be more productive and positive.

- *THE BIG BAD WORLD*: You can be dedicated to the positivity of co-creation and still understand the importance of bearing witness to the destruction and suffering in the world. Being an ally and an activist for the causes that matter to us is a wonderful thing to do with our time – but it can be very hard to understand how best to protect our precious attention when it comes to true horror that happens in the world. This is something I've struggled with personally. I'm the host of a podcast called *The Deep*, which primarily shares stories of unthinkable trauma and the people who have overcome it. So, I'm often exposed to the pain and suffering, injustice and outrage in the world today. As I'm writing this, many of us are grappling with the unthinkable atrocities taking place in Gaza and Sudan. We watch in horror, feeling helpless to effect change. We can feel the impact that the news is having on our nervous systems, our mental health, and yet we do not want to turn away. And if our core values include empathy and compassion, ignoring the suffering of others goes against the principles we have chosen to live by. This is where it becomes important to be very deliberate and mindful about how we choose to consume information.

How do you consume the news? Do you read one or two reliable articles to stay informed while keeping enough mental and emotional space to ensure you can still function? Or are you doom-scrolling, watching, reading, obsessing and absorbing suffering from multiple sources all the time? I know I was. There was a time when I was unable to separate myself from the stories I was exposed to through my podcast. I was taking on vicarious trauma, living as if each of these people's stories were mine. The more I heard the more I needed to understand how these atrocities had occurred. The mind wants to make sense of these horrific acts.

And I wouldn't stop until it made sense. So, I get this. On a very deep level. I know how destructive this can be. How unhealthy for us. But I was at the mercy of a constant barrage of information, completely out of control. Are you like I was, or do you feel in control of how you choose to engage? Did you even realise you have a choice?

It's important to be informed but it's not helpful to be inundated. Being inundated stops us from being able to take action and instead it paralyses us. Being informed allows us to sit and think about how we can best be of service to this particular issue at this specific time. Is it writing to the electorate? Is it donating? Is it turning up to assist in charity work or to attend rallies? It is very hard to make these decisions when our nervous system is in fight-or-flight mode, or when we are living vicariously through the trauma of others.

Which things do deserve our attention and why?

- **REAL LIFE**: Your home, children, partner, pets, rent or mortgage all need your precious attention. We need to make sure that our basic needs are met. But often we forget how incredible everyday life is when we are striving for more, rushing on to the next thing, when we are in 'doing mode'. Everyday life can be made beautiful with very little shifts of our attention. The gratitude you have for your home, the connection you have with your partner, the food you put on the table, the love you get to give and receive from your kids or pets: all of these things are worth paying attention to. Even in a cost of living crisis, you have been able to make it work. Meeting our basic needs and those of our family deserves our attention and our gratitude. Don't take the basics for granted – find joy in the everyday.

- ***THINGS THAT FEEL GOOD***: Things that make us feel good and that have a positive impact on our lives are well worth our precious attention. The grass beneath your feet, cooking a delicious meal, playing with your kids, getting a massage, enjoying a gorgeous glass of wine with your favourite friend – all of these simple pleasures deserve our precious attention! Make time for the little things that make life beautiful: a good coffee (or sticky chai), a long walk, taking a bath, reading. There's nothing better after a long day than getting into bed with a great book.

- ***POSITIVITY***: Surround yourself with people who make you feel good about yourself and the wider world. After reading this, you will be so much more aware of who brings positivity into your life and who doesn't. Make time for the people who make you feel good. I promise you are making them feel good too. If you have a colleague who inspires you, invite them for a wine. Spend time checking in on what your riisers are doing and draw inspiration and a plan from their success. When you're online, instead of doom scrolling or looking at influencers who make you feel less than, ask friends for recommendations on inspiring and educational content, but also for great meme or comedy accounts that make you laugh. When it comes time to unwind with some TV, I am a sucker for *Real Housewives*, which might seem counterintuitive since it's full of drama and badly behaved people. But I find it fascinating and hilarious, and it makes me feel good! Check how what content you consume makes you feel. I love horror, but I can't watch scary movies because of how stressed they make me. That's their purpose, but it doesn't feel good for me. So, I opt for watching inspiring documentaries about amazing people that have done incredible things. Or *Real Housewives*.

- ***PASSIONS AND INTERESTS***: Exploring potential passions and interests is a great place to invest our precious attention. Recently, I've tried pottery and I'm about to start painting. At times, I've put my passions and interests on the backburner to prioritise work, or the kids. But I've learned that participating in something purely for fun and with no outcome in mind is paramount for personal growth, creativity and connecting to the present. Since when was fun just for kids or dudes playing golf? So, whether it's a book club, writing poetry, or playing a team sport, make your passions a priority and give them some of your precious attention.

- ***SERVING OTHERS***: Serving others is powerful. Whether you choose to volunteer for a charity, community cause, or help out at the local school, being of service is a wonderful thing to give your time and attention to. Instead of letting the devastating state of the world crush you, devote some of your time to volunteering, raising money or rallying for a charity, contributing to a cause you believe in, or helping a friend or family member in need. Being of service is one of the most important and fulfilling parts of life.

Let me be clear: being deliberate with how to spend our precious attention is not about ignoring the things we don't like about our lives, or the world. It's SUPER important to be informed and to be honest with ourselves about problems we are facing and the state of the world we live in. But we need to consciously decide how much of our finite teapot of attention is being hijacked by an algorithm online, by intrusive thoughts and people, and by spiralling worries about things that we can't control. As you now know, I have a tendency to vicariously take on trauma that is not mine. I need to be mindful after I have consumed distressing information or spent a lot of time holding space for a friend or family member. I make a conscious effort to recalibrate back into a more balanced and spacious mindset, not just for my own sake but for my children and my home and my work. If I want to be thoughtful, patient and calm with my family, I need to be responsible for what I am mentally and emotionally consuming so that I can to show up in the way they deserve me to show up. This realisation was the reason I decided that I couldn't work on *The Deep* full time anymore. I have done my duty in that field – and left behind a legacy of hundreds of episodes that I hope will help others process their own trauma – but the cost to my mental health and the impact on my family was too high. I decided to direct my precious attention to other things. Remember, you are responsible for your boundaries and where your precious attention goes.

This work will never ask you to ignore the world – it's important to be a fully informed and aware member of society. Co-creation doesn't ask us to put our heads in the sand. But it requires us to respond to the darkness, as well as the light and beauty of life. Because life *is* beautiful and that deserves our attention too!

Meditation

Meditation can have profound positive impacts on our mental health, but it's also an essential tool for your co-creation practice. We meditate to create a conscious foundation that is robust and supportive for our very intense and overwhelming lives. It teaches us to refocus the mind, body and breath and gives us space to get honest with ourselves about what's percolating under the surface. It allows space for whatever our subconscious mind may want us to explore.

When we're busy or disconnected, we are often unaware of what's going on internally. And when we're co-creating, we need to be clear and honest with ourselves about our intentions, our desires, our dreams, and where we're at in the moment.

Meditation is a self-love practice that will support us in our manifestation: the more we love ourselves and feel deserving of what we're asking for, the faster our manifestations appear. But meditation can be challenging to begin with. I'm right with you there – I'm currently learning how to practice vedic or 'trans-cendetal' meditation, and it isn't easy. It can be incredibly uncomfortable being still. And whether you already have a medi-tation practice, or you find the idea of meditation intimidating, it's always good to come back to basics. My meditation practice always brings me back into alignment so that I can co-create effectively and without blocks.

Try to find some time to do the following meditation before you proceed to the next section – or use the QR code at the back of the book to try out the audio version, as well as some other meditations I have created just for you.

A MEDITATION FOR CO-CREATION

Whether you've never meditated before or you're a meditation master, my go-to mediation will help drop you into alignment for co-creation. It's what I call a 'mini-medi', meaning it's short and sweet, and even the busiest person can find the time for it. Find a comfortable seated position and get ready to connect with yourself and your higher power.

Close your eyes.

Take a deep breath in through your nose, filling up your lungs and taking the breath into your belly.

Hold this breath for a beat, and then exhale slowly through your mouth, releasing any tension or sound. Be mindful of your breath and how it feels. Start to connect to your body and release any tension that's in your head, neck, shoulders and jaw. Scan your body and see if there's anywhere else that tension needs to be released.

Take a few breaths here. If there are sites of tension, breathe it out as you imagine a golden orb of light emanating from the centre of your chest and melting all the tension away.

Continue to breathe slowly and mindfully.

The breath is all we need right now. Listen to your breath, inhale and exhale.

Inhale and exhale.

If your mind wanders, gently bring it back to focus on your breath. It is natural for the mind to be distracted, especially if this is a new experience. Give it grace. And reconnect to your breath.

Notice what thoughts are interrupting you. What is trying to be heard? Kindly acknowledge these thoughts and bring your attention back to your breath. Your breath is your guiding force. Your breath is all you need right now.

Are there any sensations that are nagging for your attention? Breathe into these and let them go. Come back to your breath.

With every breath in we are connecting to ourselves, to the present moment, and we are calling in peace and release.

With each breath out we are releasing any stress, letting go of negative thought loops and tension in the body.

Take another deep breath and hold for three seconds, then exhale. Repeat this three times.

Slowly start to move your fingers and toes – you may want to take a gentle stretch. When you feel ready, place your hand on your heart and open your eyes.

Take a moment to feel deep gratitude for yourself. For your body and your mind. Be thankful that you prioritised yourself, and gave yourself the gift of stillness.

Check in with yourself. How do you truly feel? Was it a challenge? If so, that's perfectly natural. If it was easy, you may be ready for a deeper, more challenging meditation practice.

See if you can start to integrate this practice into your routine. It will change your life.

Meditation is a practice, you have to work at it, and although it can be uncomfortable at first, you will soon start to see all the ways in which it supports you and your co-creation.

It's okay for thoughts to come and go – just bring yourself back to your breath. When I meditate, I just let whatever wants to pop up from my subconscious pop up, no judgement. Be patient with yourself – getting frustrated doesn't serve us, there is no perfection in meditation. Discomfort is a sign that the *new* you is challenging the *old* you. And this is expected, there will be moments you feel shaky, angry and impatient. Having this knowledge will allow you to soften when these moments arrive. Give yourself grace, space, and acknowledge these feelings and they will pass.

We have *thousands* of thoughts per day. And so many of our thoughts are just the unhelpful chatter of our busy brains. When we begin to catalogue our thoughts and really pay attention to our inner voice, we are sometimes shocked to discover that so many of our thoughts are negative, entitled or mean. It's important to be gentle with yourself as you start your meditation practice – when you're alone with all those thoughts.

It's impossible to completely avoid negative thoughts and feelings – that is totally unrealistic. But, we *can* adopt more helpful thoughts and beliefs that over time become dominant and easier to connect with. And when we change our thoughts and beliefs, we change our actions and habits . . . which changes our lives.

Oftentimes, it is in meditation that we encounter those parts of ourselves which require healing and love. Old wounds and traumas that we have not healed will make themselves known. It is important that we have compassion and patience for these parts of ourselves, and remember that we deserve the support we need to heal. You are not 'getting in the way' when you take time to heal. You're not slowing down the co-creation process.

It's the opposite, and it's essential. You are actually clearing the way for co-creation to take place. So please be mindful. If big things come up for you, seek therapy or find a friend who can support you and the healing that you need.

Prioritising healing our traumas is beneficial to us in so many ways. Not only does it allow us to let go of those unhelpful memories and beliefs from our past, it also helps us to develop a skill set that will facilitate our ability to process and move through all the future challenges and pain that life will inevitably bring. It creates resilience. Over time, we learn to find calm and clarity even in the most chaotic and upsetting moments, or shortly after the dust has settled.

We will never reach a point where we feel we have no more work to do within. Learning and healing is a lifelong and continual practice. We don't graduate. In fact, it's often the case that the greater your life becomes, and the more you 'level up', the more new challenges there are to meet.

The most important part is that we turn up every day; we show up fully, every time, with gratitude. Things will start to feel easier and make more sense, and that is something to celebrate. Don't wait to co-create until you feel you have a sense of completion – this will never arrive. You are ready right now. So, what do you really want?

Visualisation and Priming

We've discussed the power of affirmation and meditation, but another tool we have in our toolkit is *visualisation*. Visualisation is all about using the power of our minds to picture what it is we want to call in: to see what it might look like before it arrives. It can help prepare us for things that have yet to take place, and it sends the universe a strong message about how we want something we've asked for to look and feel.

Visualisation is the practice of deliberately imagining what our desired reality looks like, what it feels like, what it smells and sounds and tastes like. It is a very potent way to manifest. Have you ever rehearsed what a big meeting or presentation at work would be like? Seeing everyone sitting in front of you, slight butterflies in your stomach. Walking up to the front of the room and taking a deep breath, saying your lines. And then imagining everyone clapping and knowing you nailed the presentation? This is visualisation. Maybe you have done it with fantasies of walking down the aisle to a perfect partner or driving your dream car. All of this is visualisation.

The power of visualisation is that it gives you clarity about the intention you have set for yourself and what you want to co-create, and it prepares your body for how it will feel when you receive what you've asked for.

FYI

We know a lot about what happens to our brain when we visualise. Multiple scientific studies have shown that the same areas of the brain that are activated when we have an experience in real life are also activated when we visualise or imagine these experiences.[10] Furthermore, the feel-good chemicals – or neurotransmitters – that are released in our brains when we experience something positive

---

10 Nadine Dijkstra and Stephen M. Fleming, 'Subjective signal strength distinguishes reality from imagination' *Nature Communications* 14(1) (23 March 2023).

are also released (albeit to a lesser extent) when we *imagine* or anticipate something positive happening to us.[11]

It's no surprise that athletes are some of the greatest visualisers around, and they reap the rewards in the real world. Muhammad Ali, considered the greatest boxer of all time, said, 'If my mind can conceive it and my heart can believe it, then I can achieve it.' And he's not wrong – there have been some studies that have shown that our bodies respond to our thoughts physically. One fascinating 2004 study showed that just *thinking* about contracting a muscle can actually increase muscle strength. Participants were divided into three groups: the first group performed 'mental contractions' by imagining they were flexing certain muscles, the second group did actual muscle contractions, and the third group – the control group – did nothing. While the control group showed no improvement, the group who did the exercises increased their muscle strength by 53%. And what about our visualisers? They increased the strength of the targeted muscle by an impressive 35%![12] You may often hear athletes or gym bros call it 'mental rehearsal', but it's all the same thing. Now *imagine* what else we can achieve when we tap into the power of our minds.

For some people visualising is really easy and for others it takes time and practice. But when we are deliberate in our visualisations, it can fast track our manifestations and make us feel

11   F. da Silva Alves *et al*, 'Dopaminergic modulation of the human reward system: A placebo-controlled dopamine depletion fMRI study' *Journal of Psychopharmacology* 25(4) (2011), pp 538–549.

12   Vinoth K. Ranganathan *et al*, 'From mental power to muscle power: Gaining strength by using the mind' *Neuropsychologia* 42(7) (2004), pp 944–956.

more confident about what we need to do to bring them to life. Visualising tells the universe: I am ready to receive.

For example, if you're hoping to co-create a fantastic dinner party but you're feeling nervous about how the night will go, try picturing yourself in the kitchen going through each step of the recipe you've chosen in your mind: chop every vegetable, add every ingredient. And then imagine the faces of your loved ones as they taste the food, see everyone laughing and talking and having a great time. When it comes time to answer the door to your guests, you'll feel prepared – you've done this all before in your head – and your relaxed and confident attitude will set your friends and family at ease.

VISUALISATION

Here is a simple visualisation that *feels* really good.

First, get yourself into a really comfortable position just like you would to meditate. Place your palms facing up, relax your body, take three deep breaths.

Now, think of that thing you're truly wanting to manifest. Let's use the example of a lover or life partner. I want you to start to feel what it would be like to be in their presence.

In the early days there are feelings of desire and the excitement of the unknown, the mystery. It feels thrilling. You're overflowing with anticipation and exhiliration. There's the anticipation of the first time you touch hands, your first kiss, the first time you hold each other and your first time being intimate. And with all this excitement there's all of that human stuff that comes up too, like whether they are going to call after the first date, whether they like you as much as you like them, whether you're ready, whether you're willing. Maybe there is trepidation and low levels of fear. Feeling all of this creates an immense amount of vulnerability, but this is also a normal part of falling in love. These are all powerful feelings to work through and when I say 'work' I mean 'feel'. Feel it all. It's going to be obvious here if there are any blocks (make note of them for later), but we want our visualisations to feel good. We want them to be preparing us for the real thing.

Visualise what it would look like having this person in your space, on your couch, in your bed, that awkward moment someone needs to poop for the first time (ridiculous but true), them making themselves a cup of tea in your kitchen, making you one too, bringing it over to you on the lounge as you snuggle in to watch a movie.

Visualise what it's like when you start sharing this person with others in your life. This may bring up feelings that are more confronting. Visualise introducing them to your friends – maybe you have a little bit of tightness in your chest anticipating whether they'll like each other: what do your friends think, what does your partner think of your friends?

These are all very real moments.

Visualise the time when the honeymoon period is over and things become a little bit more everyday and comfortable. What is it like, discussing combining finances, moving in together? These are very big and foreign experiences in a new relationship whether or not you have been here with someone else before. Now, what does a normal Sunday morning look like waking up together? Imagine walking up to the cafe to eat some poached eggs on toast and then hopping into the car for a fun day out driving up the coast to the beach, having an adventure together. Start to visualise yourself already having this experience, what it's like calling them when you finish work – what it's like receiving their texts throughout the day.

Feel the feeling of knowing you're the one, that they are your one. That you have found them. Your life partner.

The power of visualisation is that it prepares your mind, your nervous system, your body and soul, for the arrival of this thing you want. Visualising is one of the most *fun* parts of manifestation; it's where we truly get to stretch what is possible and make space for what is arriving.

There is another level of visualising that we have touched on above. This is my favourite step in the process. It's called *priming*. It's very close to visualisation, but with more detail, and more attention to each little step.

I love priming because it is *fun*. And so much of the work we've done so far is hard work, so it's nice to get into the exciting stuff. If visualisation is using our imagination to convince our *minds*, priming is using our imagination to convince our *bodies*. It's linking the potency of our visualisation to our body and our physical experience. We are *feeling* the reality of a manifestation before it arrives. You may want to read that sentence again. We are behaving as if we have what we want; we are living, breathing, walking, eating as if its already happened. Priming is the process of embodying how might we feel if we already had the thing that we are trying to manifest, experience or co-create.

When someone visualises falling in love, their brain imagines how it might feel. We can evoke emotions – desire, lust, longing, fulfilment – solely through the power of our minds as if it were really happening. This visualisation in our mind stimulates a reaction in the body – and this is what we call priming. It is priming our nervous system, our minds and our physical bodies for what we wish to receive. When we are both visualising something in our mind *and* priming our bodies and nervous systems, we are, in a sense, legitimately experiencing something. And because we feel as if we have experienced our manifestation being fulfilled, it no longer feels out of reach, so hard to get. And feeling as though it has already happened leads to a wonderful feeling of embodied gratitude.

Another way I like to engage with this technique is through what I call 'priming walks'. Because priming is about feeling in the physical body, I like to go for a walk in nature and use it as an opportunity to feel the reality of this manifestation coming true. I simply take a walk as though I am already the person who has fallen in love, found financial ease, moved into my dream house . . . or whatever the focus of my manifestation may be.

Let's stay with the example of falling in love, because it's one of the things we feel most strongly in our bodies. As you walk, imagine preparing yourself for the first date. What will you wear? How will you do your hair? What perfume or cologne might you spray? Feel what it's like to get ready for this date – getting ready for your yoga class feels different in the body compared to the date. Your focus is not on the actions but how each of the actions makes you feel. How will you arrive to the date? Will you walk or drive, take the train or a taxi? Where will you go? Your favourite restaurant or a cosy cafe, maybe it's a wine at your place? Each setting conjures a very specific feeling. Imagine the moment the bill arrives (if you're out) and it's time to decide who's going to pay. Is there a little awkwardness here? Little details help. Are you going to a movie, an art gallery or a concert after? Do they reach over and touch your arm? Feel the excitement in your chest. What might they look like? How will you feel when you first see them? What will you discuss? What will you eat and drink? Imagine the sparks flying, the connection beginning, the sense of excitement building. Imagine the laughter and the resonance, imagine what it feels like to hold hands, or even to kiss. What might the goodbye look like? Is there a sense of anticipation for the next date?

The more that we can imagine and feel and the more we can *experience* this date in our minds and bodies, the clearer and more direct our request to the universe will be. This feeling, this priming, is preparing your nervous system, your mind, your body for what's coming. This mental rehearsal is getting you in the perfect condition to receive. *This*, we are saying, *all of this is what I want; specifically these things, these feelings.* The incredible thing about priming is that it's as if you had actually walked to the cinema or gone to the restaurant – that is how powerful our minds are.

I have been known to actually drive the route to a new job I'm manifesting, or get into the bed at an open home to really feel what it would be like to live in the home I wanted. Was it bonkers? Yes. Did I tell anyone? No. But I got the job – and the house! I've been using this technique for years and it's my favourite one by far.

If there are people in your life who are also co-creating, consider priming together. Try a priming call: it might feel ridiculous at first but it's so fun. Prep your friend before you call so they are ready to respond with the most potent energy. Call and explain the perfect date you had, tell them about everything you saw and felt in your priming experience. Have a conversation with this person as though it were real. Go into the details, have fun! Celebrate it! Accept their congratulations and excitement for you. *Feel* it. This is teaching your nervous system what it *feels* like to live this romantic experience. This is priming. And it is a magnet to your manifestations.

Aligned Action

Aligned action is something you've heard me mention in these pages already, but I want to make sure it's really clear – because aligned action is a critical part of co-creation. The universe has your back, but this practice of aligned action requires you to turn up mentally and energetically in order for your manifestations to arrive.

Imagine you're manifesting a new love into your life, the person you visualised meeting in the previous section. You've set your intention, you've explored how it relates to your beliefs and core values, and you're already in the right mindset to co-create. But now it's time to think about how you can actually *be* open to love, what *actions* you can take to make sure that you're ready to receive love when it arrives.

A great way to start is by making a list of what you can offer as a partner: identify the qualities you already have and are grateful for, those amazing things about you that will help you to bring love into your life. If you have trouble starting, ask a friend to help. Are you a kind person? Do you have a great sense of humour? Are you trustworthy and reliable? Take a moment to feel pride for all of the wonderful things about yourself.

Now comes the confronting part. Ask yourself: Are there any areas for improvement? Think carefully about anything that might get in the way of you and your love.

If, for example, you know you struggle with trust issues, now is the time to take action and see a therapist to heal those parts of yourself. And if finding time for dating is a problem for you, think about why that might be – are you giving too much of your precious time to your work, friends and family, and not leaving enough time to meet someone? Come up with some ways to make room in your life for your co-creation, whether that is dropping a social commitment that isn't bringing you joy, or asking for additional resources at work if you're feeling overwhelmed and find yourself putting in too much overtime.

If the issue is that you're lacking confidence and haven't even put yourself out there yet, taking aligned action to address this might look like working on repeating positive affirmations (creating new neural pathways) to shift limiting beliefs, and then signing up for a few dating apps. You could even ask a friend to help you create your online profile. If the apps aren't your thing, you could try a speed dating night. Or simply open yourself up to meeting a stranger at a bar or restaurant. Find the aligned action that feels right for you. But don't stall, do something.

Aligned action can be simply using your words with intention: start telling people you are really, truly ready to find 'the one', and express confidence and excitement about finding them. The action of saying this aloud is powerful – and you might be surprised how things unfold, maybe you will get set up with a friend of a friend who is perfect for you!

The important thing here is that you are *doing* something. That you are both looking seriously at the blocks that are in your way, and taking steps towards what you want. Find a riiser – look for someone who has a relationship you really respect, learn how they met, how they communicate and work together. You're letting the universe know you are serious and that you are matching its energy, you're not only ready for a loving partner but you are working with the universe to find one.

Rituals

All of us have routines in our life, but not all of us have rituals. A routine is practical, productive and effective, for example, waking up and brushing your teeth and then going to the gym. A ritual is intentional, mindful and symbolic. You might wake up as normal, but as soon as you add in lighting a candle, five minutes of meditation or manifestation work to your existing routine it becomes something richer – it becomes a morning *ritual*.

With little rituals sprinkled in, our days become more beautiful, and suddenly the monotony of life is given some intention and specialness. We start to find wonder in the things we take for granted all the time. Ritual connects us to gratitude and we want that punctuated throughout each and every day.

You may already have little rituals in your day that you aren't even aware of. My days are full of small moments of ritual. Every morning, I ask my kids: 'What kind of day are we going to have?' They answer, 'The best day!', or 'A fun day at the park' – they often mention something they're looking forward to. The point is, this little ritual sets intention into our day and sets us off on a positive path. Another ritual I try to stick to is finding a moment during my busy day to go out to get my sticky chai. I stop and allow myself to feel deeply grateful for the barista making my chai, and as we share a joke, suddenly another forgettable moment becomes a ritual. At night when we have dinner, I ask my children to share the best and the most challenging part of the day. It makes us all feel more connected and it gives dinner time a special sense of occasion.

ZOE'S MORNING RITUAL (THAT WILL CHANGE YOUR LIFE)

Set your alarm for 30 minutes before you normally rise. Before you're even fully awake, do a JLo. The singer famously loves affirmations, and has been known to end her morning skincare routine by saying 'It's going to be a beautiful day. I choose happiness.' You can of course use any other affirmation that resonates with you. Some of my favourites are: 'Opportunities find me', 'Everything works out for me' and 'I am a magnet for incredible people, places and things'.

Set your timer for a 5-minute meditation. You can use the QR code at the back of this book to take you to some wonderful guided meditations.

After your meditation, take a few minutes to write a gratitude list. Simmer on what you're grateful for. Really feel the gratitude in your body. For me, this can feel like warmth spreading through my chest, or as if I am being hugged by someone I love. It's a very grounding sensation.

Then for a few minutes do something that make your body feel good – stretch, move, dance, do yoga, and then start your day. Creating a small pocket of space and time for you to be in control of your mind and emotions will change your life.

Any new habit or routine can feel clunky and awkward in the beginning. When we start new habits we can feel resistance. *Why should I get up thirty minutes earlier? Why do I have to do all these things?* The answer is: you don't have to. But, if you do, you will benefit from the changes that take place.

And let's be honest, how much time do we spend scrolling on our phones or watching something mediocre on one of the twenty different streaming services we're subscribed to? This whole practice is about making choices around how you want to spend your precious attention and time. You are in control of using both the time and energy – so where you choose to direct it is up to you.

Over time, what we practise becomes habit. For example, there was probably a time when you were learning to drive and you had to constantly remind yourself what to do with all the pedals and levers – and now most of us find ourselves on auto-pilot when we drive. It has become second nature. Eventually, co-creation and all the practices that it encompasses will too.

Rituals are a wonderful way to integrate co-creation into your life. Birthdays, full moons, deaths, the start of a new year – almost all cultures have rituals around these events. But even regular Sunday nights can be a great time to introduce a ritual; taking the time to prepare for the week ahead. There are no rules. You can create your own rituals.

The point of rituals is that they are meaningful, they are intended to mark a significant transition or moment, or to celebrate an achievement, or to just mindfully connect to the universe and yourself. When you complete a ritual you should feel different from how you felt when you started it. You should feel more grounded, you should have more clarity about what you want, and you should feel in deep alignment with your intentions. While some rituals can be simple moments we take for ourselves during a busy day or week, others can be more occasional, specific and transformative. But all kinds of rituals can help us with our co-creation practice.

RITUALS

When you're ready to introduce a ritual into your life, choose a time and place that feels good. There are so many potential rituals and I encourage you to feel into which ones are right for you. Your body will be the guide to this.

Candle Rituals: Lighting a candle when you begin something and blowing it out when you finish it can turn anything into a beautiful ritual. Light a candle before you begin journalling, meditating, or your manifestation practice. Call in a feeling of peace and connect to your higher power. The candle symbolises the start and the end of something meaningful and intentional.

Embodied Bathing: Water is such a powerful element to add to rituals. This can be achieved with either a bath or a shower. Light candles, add some beautiful essential oils, play some music and connect to your physical body. Bathing in this way can be a gift of deep self-love. Whilst connected to your body, remember that it is the vessel of your life force, keeping you breathing, allowing you movement and housing your soul. Take yourself to the parts of the body you may be at war with – any points of pain or discomfort, any sources of shame. Touch these parts and make peace, give thanks and love to all parts of you, even the ones you deem flawed. Make an agreement that as you dry off from this bath or shower you are honouring this beautiful body, and each time you bathe it is with love.

Moon Rituals: I am someone who is deeply impacted by the moon. My cycle seems to sync with it and sometimes even my sleep gets impacted. The more in tune you start to become with yourself the more you will begin to notice the impact of the world around you on your mind and body, from the changing seasons to the cycle of the moon. There's also an undeniable connection between manifestation and the lunar cycle. It can be helpful to learn about the phases of the moon and what they signify, and use the lunar cycle to your advantage when manifesting. A new moon can be the perfect time to set an intention because it represents potential and new beginnings. A full moon, on the other hand, is perfect for letting go of things that are holding you back.

Fire Rituals: Fire rituals can help us banish bad energy from our lives. If you are processing trauma and need a release, write your feelings down on paper. Whether it is sadness, anger, disappointment or feelings of betrayal, go into as much detail as you can – no matter how ugly it gets – and let yourself really feel it. When you have nothing left to say, *burn it*. Releasing negative emotions through fire is a powerful transmutation – turn the rage or sadness into clarity and strength. Let it go. Let the universe take your hurt and replace it with trust.

Most of us need evidence and rewards to help us commit to something new. So, when starting a new ritual or habit, reflect on how you feel. How has it has changed your day or your week? Do you feel more connteced to yourself and your manifestations? You are more likely to commit to a ritual long term if you are motivated by your rewards or results.

Storytelling

It can be illuminating to look at our lives like a story. What is the story so far? Who are the main characters? How did the story begin? How has it changed over the years . . . and where do you want it to go next?

The stories we tell ourselves impact our lives and shape how our life unfolds. This is further proof that we truly are the authors of our life, and that is empowering.

Us beautiful humans have a range of emotions and feelings to help us interpret and perceive the world around us. The stories we tell ourselves are made up of many aspects of our lives woven together: how we were raised, where we were raised, the people we know and love, our lived experiences and our traumas. When we attach strong emotions to these stories, we form beliefs. We might say, 'I'm a failure; bad things always happen to me,' or, 'Manifesting only works for other people, but it won't work for me.' If these stories are challenged, we may defend them by saying, 'Well, this is the way things have always been for me. Why would things change?' But this can keep us stuck in a place we don't want to be. It can cause us to avoid responsibility for our own futures and make us feel powerless. When this happens, our stories have become what I call 'core limiting beliefs'.

For example, let's say you were raised in a family like mine where there was constant financial hardship. Your parents constantly argued about money and you were told as a child that there was never enough cash to get by. What happens? You learn that money is scarce and a source of unease, and you believe this as if it were an objective fact. And when you see that other people do have money and seem to have a healthier relation-ship with it, you assume that it is your unworthiness that keeps you in lack, and that you don't deserve it. But this is just a *story* about money, one you learned as a very small child. It's an interpretation, not a fact, but if you have known no other way, it can become your truth.

Now, imagine you were raised in a very different family environment. One where not only were your needs met financially, but money was never a block to what you desired and it always felt like there was enough. This would mean that in those crucial, formative years when you were developing what would later become your beliefs and your story, you were shown that money is everywhere, all your needs were met and you were worthy of it. You learned that money is used to access opportunities and that there is enough for everyone. You *know* that money is always there and will always support you. This is also just a story. It is also just a belief. But it is a much more advantageous story to tell yourself because it sends a powerful signal to the universe. It says: *Money comes easily, all my needs are met.* Rather than: *Money is hard and painful, I never have enough.*

I like to use money as an example because it is one that's familiar to most of us. Examining our money stories is one of the fastest ways to discover whether we hold ourselves in a place of financial worthiness and value. And because money is dominant in our society, it is a major focus in co-creation. It is one of the main things that people want to manifest.

The stories we tell ourselves about money are just one example of how our interpretation of life experiences can shape our sense of self, the world and what is possible.

We may have inherited unhelpful stories around health, careers, around relationships and love. As you truly learn that co-creation is not an activity that you dabble in occasionally – it's not something that you pick up and put down like a toy but an operating system that will restructure your mind and the way you perceive the entirety of your life – you will inevitably come up against other stories you've been telling yourself for years. Some you may choose to keep, others you might decide no longer serve you.

Most of us are familiar with the concept of nature vs. nurture. It asks us to explore what qualities and characteristics are the result of nature (genetic predispositions) and what are the results of nurture (how we were raised). Now, we all know there is no 'money gene'! Of course, if you come from a wealthy family and have plenty of help to pursue education or even to buy a house, you will find yourself in a better financial position than someone who hasn't had these privileges in early life. But even if you *haven't* had those privileges, there is nothing that is stopping you from taking control and manifesting financial abundance. Your 'nurturing' may have convinced you that you can't be financially secure, but your 'nature' – your inherent ability to manifest – is no different from someone who has grown up with all that they need. It's the stories we tell ourselves that determine whether we have a scarcity mindset or a mindset of abundance. And our mindset determines what we attract into our lives.

One of the reasons we resist giving up limiting stories is that they have become coping mechanisms. By giving us a sense of control, of being able to predict what will happen, they can help us deal with stress or trauma. They help us feel safe by telling us what to expect from life, but if left unchecked they can create major blocks to living the life we truly want to live. I know this, because I lived it.

As you know, I was raised by a single mum. I watched her work herself to the bone at two jobs. I witnessed how financial stress overwhelmed her and impacted her quality of life. Some might assume that I would continue the trauma cycle and repeat my mother's experience. That I would end up divorced, working my arse off for someone else's business. That I would forever stress about money and ultimately give myself over to a life of struggle because that is what I witnessed and this was the *story* of my life.

But you know what? The opposite happened. Because even when I was still holding on to the self-limiting stories and believing society's ideas of who I should be, I knew I deserved to experience the opposite of what my mum did. I knew I deserved a loving, supportive husband that wanted to be there for my family. I knew I deserved my own financial security and to run my own successful businesses. I knew that I deserved to be with my kids all the time. To do pick-ups and drop-offs, help with canteen duty and attend school concerts and *still* make an abundant living.

So, please trust me when I say that the story you thought was yours can change. You can write a new chapter and you can decide when and how that story is written. Sometimes we just need a catalyst. My catalyst came when my mum died and I was forced to step into her financial stress, dissolve her struggling business and deal with her debt. Faced with the reality of what that financial story felt like, I was driven to experience another way. A different story.

In the same way that we have core values – positive ideas and frameworks that guide how we make decisions and engage with the world – we also possess core limiting beliefs, those negative ideas and concepts that similarly impact our decisions and behaviour. These core limiting beliefs may be based on real events, but our interpretation of these events is what really matters. This is how we create meaning and a sense of identity and purpose in our lives. One of the most effective ways to rework our core limiting beliefs is by examining them closely alongside our core values in a reasonable, sensible way so that we can really feel the incompatibility of our core values with our limiting beliefs.

Go back and look at the section on core values (p. 32), and revisit your own list. If you determined that kindness and generosity are important values for you, then these values should influence how you choose to behave, and how you treat others. And when you treat others with kindness and generosity, or remove yourself from situations that feel unkind or ungenerous, you are living these values. But you might also have a limiting belief that the universe won't provide you with the things and experiences that your heart truly wants. Perhaps you believe you aren't worthy or good enough to deserve the generosity and kindness of the universe. Can you see that these two belief systems can't co-exist? It's like ordering a package of abundance and just as the package hits your door step, your doubts and fears act as a 'return to sender' label saying, 'Nope, this can't be for me!' But if you perceive kindness and generosity within yourself, the universe will offer kindness and generosity back to you. You just have to be ready to receive it.

There is a concept that I have found to be so healing and so effective when it comes to the rerouting of our neural pathways so that we can accept new stories about the world and ourselves. It's called 're-parenting' or 'parenting ourselves'. There is a clinical form of re-parenting that involves working with a therapist, and if this is something that resonates with you, I recommend you seek out this specific type of healing. But there is also a DIY version that I want to offer you now. The simplest framework for understanding re-parenting is that we, as adults, determine what needs were unmet by our parents when we were children, and we find ways to meet those needs for ourselves, now.

I want to focus specifically on re-parenting when it comes to the messages we received from our parents around worthiness and value, which are directly linked to our ability to co-create. Re-parenting in this context involves another term you may already be familiar with: the inner child.

If you sense that worthiness, imposter syndrome, doubt and worry have become deeply embedded into the story you tell yourself *about* yourself, then it's time to tune in to your inner child. Ask your inner child what they believe about themselves, about life, about abundance, about their own power. Ask them why they believe these stories, where they learned them from, and whether those beliefs feel good. Ask them if they would like to learn a new story. Ask them if they'd like to feel better about themselves and their place in the world. Ask them if they'd like to learn to co-create with the universe.

Be patient, give your inner child the time and space they may need to respond. And, when they do, invite them to join you on this path. They are a huge key to accessing your self-worth. If it feels right, listen to what they need from you to heal. Share with them the core values you have now, and the manifestations you are calling in. I promise your inner child wants the same love, peace and connection you want today.

Begin to notice how these new stories and beliefs feel inside your body, what emotions begin to arise. See whether doubt and worry cause you to step back, or if joy and excitement push you to step forward, and consider how your life can begin to change. Write down what you have learned from your inner child. Has it revealed some new insights about yourself? Has it shown you ways to heal the parts of you that were desperate to be seen and heard? Writing down the impacts of these exercises helps us reflect and build evidence that they work and are worth doing. Collecting evidence is a really important part of this process, as we must work to replace the beliefs that the world works against us, that we are unlovable or unworthy. Soon, you will have a new set of experiences and plenty of evidence of your own growth and worth.

Pride Lists

When we're co-creating, it's important that we treat ourselves with empathy, grace and patience: we have to become our own best friend, safe place, and biggest cheerleader. And one of the easiest and most impactful ways we can build up our self-worth is with a pride list. A pride list is created to remind us of all that we have achieved (big or small) and it has so many positive impacts: it helps us develop our self-worth, it reminds us of our courage and resilience, and it tracks our personal growth in a very practical and effortless way.

Pride lists highlight what we should be proud of, even the little things that we may take for granted or skim over. They allow us to really feel how amazing we are. And they are especially helpful on those days where we feel like the messy and uncomfortable middle might be the messy and uncomfortable *forever*, because they remind us how far we have come.

Writing a pride list is simple, although it isn't always easy. Start by jotting down five things you are proud of. These could be tiny things you may see as insignificant, all the way up to big, life changing moments and achievements. Refer to this list three times a day (setting an alarm can help), feeling into each point for one minute. Really feel into it, let the pride fill you.

Add a new point of pride each day, bumping off the one at the top of the list so there are always five.

ZOE'S PRIDE LIST

1. Today, I had a really difficult conversation with a client at work. I was able to stay calm but firm. Even though it was uncomfortable, I stood my ground and got a great result.

2. I went for a jog today. I started with 30 seconds jogging followed by 30 seconds of walking. I pushed past a self-limiting belief that I'm not good at running, and I fought the urge to give up after a few minutes. I'm proud of setting myself up for success with a realistic way to start. I'm taking care of my health and fitness.

3. I set a boundary today with a family member. It was really uncomfortable, something I am not used to doing, but it needed to be done. I am so proud I found the courage and followed through even though I was nervous. I am prepared if that boundary needs to be reinstated. I can see how much self-growth is happening.

4. I called a friend, we laughed and talked about the next time we're going to catch up. I have deep connections with people in my community, I am loved, I am worthy.

5. I put myself to bed early tonight and read my book. I'm giving myself self-care, nourishment and nurturing. An early night is going to set me up to be in a better frame of mind tomorrow.

When you have those five things down on the page and you are reading over them, the trick is to not just mindlessly rattle them off, but rather to simmer on the meaning and feeling. What did you have to overcome to achieve each item on your list? How did it feel when you did it? Each pride point needs its moment in the sun to remind you that you can do hard things. You have been there before and you can do it again.

Whether it's pushing yourself during a workout or setting a boundary with someone close to you, acknowledge what you have done and what it took to achieve it. As you remember these moments during your day, you are creating new neural pathways and reinforcing your self-esteem. Writing pride lists will help you feel that you are deserving of all your co-creations.

You will get used to looking for things to feel proud of, you'll get better at articulating them and feeling their importance. The most exciting part of this is the way it shapes and creates new positive beliefs, ingraining them into the body, the nervous system and the mind. You never outgrow a pride list. I still do mine every day.

Micro-manifestations

When we start this work, most of us are hoping to manifest big things in our lives. We want that promotion, that new love, that red Ferrari. But learning to tune into the smaller ways the universe is responding to our vibration can also be extremely rewarding. Micro-manifestations are a great way to build evidence that co-creation works, and to increase your confidence and audacity as you call in greater manifestations.

I call these smaller (and often faster) co-creations 'micro-manifestations'. When we manifest something that is smaller and more accessible, we can see the co-creation process work on a smaller scale. And a micro-manifestation can be a *big* confidence booster and evidence creator.

We've all had micro-manifestations, even if we didn't know that's what they were at the time. Finding the perfect car spot in a crowded car park when you really needed it; thinking about someone and then bumping into them out of the blue; wanting a new jacket and then seeing that exact one on sale in the window of a store you don't usually walk past. These are all micro-manifestations. And they can turn up energetically as well as physically. Micro-manifestations can come in the form of finding a resource or support when you are feeling really stuck, calling in ease and flow at a time of high stress, or even a smile from a stranger. These micro-manifestations all symbolise that you are energetically primed. That you are 'high vibe'. So even if you haven't specifically asked for anything other than 'ease and flow', you are aligned with the universe and magnetic to what you're feeling. Sceptics might call them coincidences – but there is no coincidence in co-creation.

Micro-manifestations can also help us tune into the feelings or experiences we're seeking. They can teach us to focus less on the specifics of the manifestation and more on the feelings it produces. For example, maybe you've been feeling very overwhelmed and haven't had enough time for self-care, and you're asking the universe to provide you with more space. You are being specific about the feeling you want to achieve, while trusting the universe to decide what that looks like. Then, perhaps a dear friend brings you something delicious to eat, or you win a gift certificate for a spa day, or maybe you experience a series of cancellations that give you unexpected time to self-nurture in bed with a good book.

Micro-manifestation can help us become more open and receptive to the beautiful opportunities coming our way. We might ask for something as small and simple as a little more joy, ease, opportunity or delight. And the universe will surprise us in how it brings that feeling into our life. We become magnets for more connected and meaningful moments with people, more time, more money, more opportunity. And as your micro-manifestations start to appear, they will add to all the evidence you've been gathering that this practice works.

The process of micro-manifesting is no different from the way you approach those bigger manifestations: set your intentions, feel or visualise the outcome, take aligned action, trust the process and celebrate the arrival of your manifestation when it comes. The only difference is that you're asking for something small: that last-minute cancellation at your favourite restaurant that is always booked out, or a little self-esteem boost in the form of a compliment from a stranger. The benefit of micro-manifestation is to be able to really track the connection between the asking or feeling and the receiving. These micro-manifestations build confidence and trust and prepare you for the big audacious co-creations to come.

The Switch

It's time to introduce 'The Switch'.

The Switch is the shift *away* from negative thought patterns and feelings and *towards* positive ones. It takes awareness, dedication, and perseverance to keep coming up against old limiting beliefs and to switch them to ones that support our greater good. But making this switch is necessary for successful co-creation.

So, how do you make the Switch? This section will give you all the tools you need to make the switch in your everyday life. You just need the awareness and willingness to commit to it.

The Switch begins with rewiring your thoughts and emotions through deliberate practices and new habits that reinforce the positivity around you. Think about the city or town that you live in. Now think about the places you usually visit each week: work, the supermarket, school, the gym. Most of us follow the same routes to and from these destinations every time, so often that we can make that drive from home to work without even thinking about it – we are on autopilot. This is just like a neural pathway. They are the embedded patterns that our thoughts follow. And like the route from home to work, we repeat them mindlessly, because they no longer need our awareness – they are embedded and part of the programming.

When we talk about rewiring our thoughts or establishing new neural pathways, it's a bit like deciding that you're going to take a different route to work. Perhaps you'll choose some back roads that take you through a different area. And along this new route you'll notice different things. A new cafe you may want to try, different stores you'd like to visit, a beautiful florist. You may ask, 'Was this here all along? How did I miss it?' A whole new way of seeing the world and the opportunities within it opens up when we change our way of doing things, impacting our neural pathways and rewiring our thought patterns. And just like it takes deliberate action and intention to drive to work along a new route, it takes deliberate action and intention to make the Switch.

You already have so many tools in your toolkit that will help you make the Switch. Everything we've explored together so far will support you in creating these new pathways: meditation, affirmations, gratitude, mindfulness with your precious attention and pride lists . . . all of these practices are for your greater good. They will help you align your vibration with the universe in such a way that you may co-create your truest desires. The Switch is about making the conscious decision to practice these things in our daily lives, especially when things aren't going our way. It's about shifting away from negativity and any limiting beliefs and towards positivity and the infinite opportunity that is everywhere.

If you're struggling with the Switch, try a circuit breaker to get you into a more positive and abundant vibration. Circuit breakers, in this context, are things that shift our attention and physical feelings away from doubt, worry, lack and scarcity, and towards fun, excitement and joy. These include dancing (and I mean dancing like no one is watching), truly expressing yourself without any self-consciousness, or doing movements that just make you feel so good. Listening to your favourite music is an immediate circuit breaker. It could be hip hop hyping you up to go into a big meeting or first date, or it could be emotional music supporting you to release sadness so you can get past a block (nothing feels better than a big cry that needs to get out!).

Walking has always been a profound way to shift energy. For most of us, it is easy and effortless and something we can do without thinking. But walking is also a way to check in with our bodies and with nature. Even on a walk around your suburb you can connect with miracle of nature, you are able change how you are feeling quite quickly through movement and awareness of the world around you. To truly ground yourself in nature, try taking your shoes off and connecting with the earth below, or sit on the beach, swim in the sea. Being with nature is medicinal. It soothes the soul.

Play or partaking in a hobby is another way to switch your energy. Playing with no outcome, no agenda, is magic. We tend to lose this ability as adults. We don't see the value in doing something with no clear purpose. Play with the kids or animals in your life and you will see that there is so much joy to be had. Or immerse yourself in comedy; watching a funny video, even if it's quick, can boost serotonin and help you make the Switch.

Reading something stimulating, or cooking a recipe that you love (and eating it!) are a few more of the almost endless ways to switch ourselves into high vibe, abundant beings. Self-pleasure is also an amazing way to shift your energy, to boost creativity and even help with headaches – it's very hard to stay in a slump after an orgasm. And it's true, I've tested it.

The Switch is the conscious decision to shift into your highest and most abundant energy. It's a choice that you keep making, day after day.

Part 4

Blocks

Everything that you have learned so far – from how to explore your thoughts and beliefs, to aligning your vibration, practicing gratitude, meditation and cultivating a mindset of abundance – all of these things are conduits for a deep and meaningful conversation with the most important person in your life: *you*. But many of us discover that when we start this conversation with ourselves, we experience blocks. A block is anything that comes between us and co-creation, anything that slows down our process, or feeds into our doubt. We're going to explore a few different kinds of blocks in this section and how to overcome them. But first I want to share a story with you about a time when I went up against just about every block in the book.

About eighteen months ago, after I'd finished a year-long renovation on our dream home, it flooded. Flooded! I remember being upstairs giving the kids a bath with the rain hammering outside. Benji was calling out from downstairs: 'It's flooded! It's flooded! I can't get the water to stop coming in!'

By the time I got the kids dried and dressed and came downstairs, he was shin deep, sloshing about in water. We were living on the first floor and downstairs was a gym and a lounge area.

I remember thinking how ridiculous the timing was that we just finished this renovation and *then* the house flooded. And in that moment, I immediately dropped into a place of gratitude; I was grateful that I had access to a phone to call emergency help, and that we had this incredible gardener that lived around the corner and who could help Benji try and figure out what was going on. I was grateful that I was home, but also that Benji was home having a meeting in the room that flooded – if he hadn't been in it when the water rose things could've been so much worse.

We both frantically called so many emergency plumbers only to find that they were busy because of the rain. I was confused in the chaos, unsure if anyone would come at all. But thankfully a plumber turned up. I was grateful we had insurance that would cover (almost) everything.

In the aftermath, a lot of things were ruined. But I also saw that as a really great opportunity to declutter. The only thing I cared about was a box of special items from my childhood with my mum – and it was okay. I just found so much to be grateful for in the process of fixing the damage.

By this time in my life, with all the co-creation work I'd been doing for years, I knew this wasn't a personal attack. It was nature (and a small release pipe on the rain water tank). Shit happens. So I chose to see what was working and anchor into gratitude, take aligned action, and focus on being intentional with my mindset and thoughts. Was it a walk in the park? No. It was a reminder that sometimes no matter what you do, things still just go wrong. It took six months to manage the water and damage. It pissed me off. And yes, it was inconvenient and the tradies were frustrating and there were fights with insurance and many more difficult things. It was a challenging time.

And, just when it seemed like things could not have gotten more stressful, I found a lump in my breast. Immediately, my thoughts went to a dark place. I couldn't help but think back to that day when my mum had told me about her own lump, and I had known deep down that she would die. I was scared. I went to the doctor and had an ultrasound. She was confident that it wasn't anything serious – at least not yet. But she told me that we would have to monitor it closely, with check-ups every six months. It was good news, but it didn't feel like it.

At this time, I was working as a content creator, or 'influencer' as some like to call it, making a lot of online content for brands. It wasn't intentional, I just kind of fell into it. The money was extraordinary and the work was easy, although I didn't love it. I was committed to my true work on my podcast *The Deep* and thought I could support my *real* work by doing the content creation. And the money got more and more ludicrous. Soon I was so overworked with content creation and saying yes to every job just because of the financial benefit. Being raised by a mother who worked two jobs on minimum wage, it felt almost disrespectful not to take the work – I felt like I couldn't turn away from this kind of opportunity when my mum had struggled so much. I had this kind of shame attached to denying an opportunity to make money.

When the flood happened, I remember I had maybe nine or ten campaigns I'd committed to for Mother's Day, and they all had to go out the same week, which in influencer land is ridiculous, it was too much paid content. Everything was so intense. And in that moment, I hated this work that I had once enjoyed. I realised that I'd kept saying yes to all of these jobs that weren't aligned with my true self, I was just being wooed by the money.

And that only created more jobs that I didn't feel aligned with, more work that I wasn't passionate about. I found myself in this cycle because I kept saying yes to this work that wasn't right for me.

With the thought of cancer still hanging over me, and all those work deadlines now catching up with me, I had an existential crisis and really hit a breaking point just after Mother's Day. I had been keeping myself so busy, distracting myself from the pain of finding the lump and the trauma triggered my safety-seeking behaviour: do *more* work to get *more* money, to be safe. I was so confused, I didn't even know who I was or what I wanted anymore. All I knew was I was trying to survive this very terrifying moment of fear around my health. And so, instead of feeling those feelings, I just continued chaotically working. It was all making me so deeply unhappy that a breakdown was inevitable.

But, from breakdowns come breakthroughs. I knew I had to make a change if I was going to get through this incredibly difficult time. And true clarity came when I started saying no. I remember calling my manager and feeling so nervous as I explained to her that I only wanted to take on jobs that really aligned with me from then on. Instead of the frustration I expected, she was supportive – I couldn't even believe how gracious and understanding she was. And then the strangest thing happened, my social media work slowed down tremendously. It was like the universe was doing the heavy lifting. Forcing me to stop. I had a couple of jobs that tested my resolve. But I realised how my higher power was supporting me and I can say, hand on heart, I haven't done a job that makes me cringe since. Stepping into this work so publicly has really required me to be incredibly clear and truthful about who I am and what I stand for. Was it comfortable? No. Was it worth it? Yes.

I may not have got a satisfying resolution about the lump in my breast – more on that later – but I had co-created some much-needed space in my life to deal with what was ahead of me. When we are confronted with something that challenges us, our first instinct is often to seek comfort and distraction. We attempt to block negative feelings with scrolling on TikTok, eating junk food, overworking, shopping online, drinking alcohol or doing drugs – whatever we think will numb us and distract us. We will do almost anything to avoid discomfort.

But sometimes what we need most is to sit with the discomfort and listen to what it's trying to tell us. Next time you're dealing with something difficult in your life, try giving yourself some time and space to do nothing. Sit with it. It's going to feel excruciating and foreign at first, but very slowly that feeling of discomfort will soften, and you will realise that it's just another feeling that will pass.

And now that you know this, you can explore that feeling, ask: What is this discomfort trying to say? What is the feeling under the discomfort? In my case, the flood, the excessive work, and even the breast lump – all of those uncomfortable, awful things – were actually trying to tell me something on a much deeper level. They were stirring up issues from my childhood and my traumatic relationship; feelings of unsafety, scarcity, instability, lack, and even painful memories about my mother's own breast cancer. My first impulse was to distract myself with more work. But what I really needed to do was pull back and sit with those dark thoughts and feelings, sit with my discomfort, and listen to what it was it trying to tell me.

This takes true courage. So few people want to venture to this place, and that's completely understandable. But it's the exploration of your discomfort that will help you identify what it is that you really need. For me, during this dark time, it certainly wasn't more work or even fixing the flood damage. It was slowing down and connecting with myself and having time to process all this big stuff that was being hurled at me from every angle. Checking in if I needed professional support. Being with my family rather than in meetings and shooting content. Being present rather than hiding in distraction so I could see the extraordinary life I had created, full of loving people who were available to support me. I now realise that I was hiding behind my busyness, adding every possible stressor to my life so I could pretend I was okay. Complete and utter madness.

One of my primary intentions with this book – and with the work I do to bring this information to the people who need it – was to create a co-creation manual, grounded in truth, that helps people meet their deepest needs with unwavering honesty. There are plenty of other books and resources out there which have oversimplified the co-creation process. And that is because there is an inherent paradox in the teachings I am presenting to you here. On the one hand, I have told you that when we align our vibration with the universe, co-creation flows easily and abundantly in the service of manifesting our dreams and desires into a physical, tangible reality. This is true. But it is also true that the universe has access to far more information about our deepest needs than we do. The universe understands what we need to experience and overcome in order to arrive at a place where we are truly ready to receive. And sometimes we have hard lessons to learn, or things that will blindside us before we can see with clarity once again.

Can this be frustrating? *Yes.* Is it a necessary part of the process? *Yes.* So, what do we do when times get tough?

Tests

Tests are opportunities we are given to settle for less than what we really want, to accept a lesser version of the manifestations that we have called in, to be sidetracked and distracted by the mirage of something that feels close enough, or good enough – because we are still uncertain about whether we deserve to receive what we really want. The content creation work that I was taking on during the flood was a test: it was something that seemed like an opportunity I was manifesting so that I'd have money and security to work on my podcast. But all it was really doing was taking all my time and attention away from that work.

For example, let's say that you have decided that you want to co-create a new job opportunity. You have expressed this want to the universe from a place of alignment and clarity. You are doing the work, clearing any blocks and showing up to participate fully in this co-creation. This aligned action might look like tailoring your CV to the role you want, setting up some alerts on job sites for the kinds of positions you have in mind, researching companies you want to work with, and finding some riisers to inspire you.

You're ready for this new opportunity to arrive, and you've taken all the right steps to make it happen. But when the job alerts start going off, they're *almost* what you want but none of them are quite right. One sounds really interesting, but it's offering a lot less money than you were hoping for. Another is part-time when you wanted something full-time. A third looks great on paper, but on further investigation you realise that the company is not aligned with your ethical values. They are all so close to what you wanted, but none of them feel right. None of them feel like a big, resounding 'yes'. And when we are in a place of self-doubt and unworthiness, we might find ourselves settling for one of these jobs. We might think, 'Maybe this is as good as it gets, it's not so bad, I just need to compromise.'

But, my friends, let me tell you: this is a test.

The universe is testing you, checking you, asking you to be clear and precise in what you want. What we say 'no' to in the co-creation process is just as important as what we say 'yes' to. We are sending the signal back to the universe: close, but not good enough. Almost there, but not quite. We will know the 'yes' when we feel it, it's strong and it's in the body – we feel it in the gut – and nothing else will do.

The universe needs clarity. Every 'No, not quite' that we offer as feedback assists the universe in getting it right. It's like going to a really expensive restaurant. You've saved up for this dinner, and you already know you want the lobster pasta. But, when the order comes out, it's not lobster – it's crab. It looks lovely, smells great, but you ordered the lobster, not the crab. Would you settle? Or send the dish back and wait for the meal that you craved, saved up for, and ordered? Lots of us would settle. We tell ourselves It's too much effort to send it back, the staff will think I'm difficult, the crab will be just fine. But should you really just let that slide? This says a lot about you. What are you willing to settle for?

Learning to be a master manifestor requires understanding what the non-negotiables are for you. You may desire to manifest a big house. And then you drive by a house with a 'For Sale' sign in front of it that, at first glance, looks perfect. But as you approach the house you notice that it has no windows – not a single window! You'd turn right back around, get in your car and drive away, wouldn't you? Windows in a house are non-negotiable.

We must be firm and clear about what we are willing to accept from the universe, just like we are firm and clear on the fact that our homes must have windows or that our pasta must have lobster. Co-creation puts tests in our way to help us learn and get clear, not to settle for good enough, or close enough. And while it can be confusing and frustrating, once we learn to recognise what's going on, it's exhilarating. It's like a master class in self-worth. Your self-worth is the key to your manifestations arriving. All of the tools we are learning are vital for navigating the tests that come our way. But they also help us overcome our deepest fears, doubts and worries.

Doubt and Worry

One of the biggest challenges we face when co-creating is how to manage doubt and worry. Let's have a moment for the shadow side of life. There is no light without darkness. There is always a shadow to every single soul you meet, to every situation. It is what makes this rich, beautiful tapestry of life.

But our shadow selves – the dark side of us, our negative thoughts and worries – are nothing to run and hide from. In fact the shadows are just sharing more helpful information about what you feel and think, they are a gateway to understanding your blocks and what parts of you don't yet feel deserving. Your shadow is part of you and needs to be welcomed in this work.

We have discussed protecting our precious attention and being hyperaware of the information and content that we consume and process. We have control over many of the things we choose to give our attention to, and where we do have control, we should enforce it. However, there are plenty of things that we do not have control over.

Our carefully orchestrated co-creation strategies can be thrown into chaos. Upsetting things can happen to the people we love, or to ourselves. World events can have a big impact on our lives, as we all experienced during the COVID-19 pandemic. To worry about our loved ones, the future, the world and ourselves is to be human. But there's worry, and then there's obsessive worry. This kind of worry feels like catastrophising, and this is something we *do* have control over.

Because my mum was a single working mother, I was raised partially by my nan. And my nan was a huge worrier. She always had something to worry about. 'Zoe,' she would say, 'don't get too comfortable or happy, anything could happen and you need to be ready.' I remember thinking, 'Ready for what, Nan?' But after a while I began to take her worry on as my own, because over-worrying is a learned behaviour. So, I adopted the hyper-vigilance my nan taught me, and I was always on guard for what 'could' happen. Naturally, worrying became my default. I would find myself worrying all the time about all those 'things' I needed to be ready for. It was exhausting.

I've worked hard at shifting my perspective away from worry. As a mum of two young kids, it can be so easy to be in a constant state of worry for them. If we're not mindful, worry can overtake us and guide our decision making. I know if I don't stay commit-ted to my morning meditation and self-care practices, I can easily slip into my old default worry mode. The beautiful thing about all of the practices and tools you are learning on this co-creation path is that they all reinforce each other: the more we practise gratitude, the easier meditation becomes; the more we track our evidence, the easier trust becomes . . . it all feeds into the same powerful place, which is our co-creative power.

Sometimes we confuse worry with doubt. They can feel very similar. Worry is focusing on what might go wrong: it's those negative 'What if?' questions that plague all of us occasionally. Doubt, on the other hand, is a lack of faith or confidence that good things will happen to us. And both worry and doubt can block co-creation: worry emits negative energy into the universe, and doubt blocks and impacts the trust we need for this process to work.

Doubt can arise from healthy scepticism, which is understandable. Scepticism makes us curious to find out more, it leads us to ask questions and gather more information so we can make informed decisions. And it's human nature to worry about things sometimes. The trouble comes when we get stuck in cycles of doubt and worry.

If we let doubt and worry run wild, they have the ability to stop us from experiencing opportunites that will help us grow. And they can blind us to all the evidence that co-creation is working. But don't worry – you already have the tools you need to manage all that doubt and anxiety. Some of my favourite techniques for fighting these feelings are asking these questions: Is this real? Is this something that needs immediate attention? Is there something I can do to remedy this?

Journalling can assist in figuring out where these doubts or worry cycles are coming from, while affirmations and meditation can be very helpful for managing these feelings when they come up.

Unworthiness and Imposter Syndrome

A funny thing happens when we start thinking about what the highest version of our life looks like, when we begin to align ourselves with a higher vibration and communicate with a higher power – God, the universe, spirit – that is conspiring for our greater good. We start to learn how we feel about ourselves. We discover whether we truly feel worthy and deserving of what we want.

The root of all blocks is unworthiness. When we don't believe we are good enough, smart enough, valuable enough, important enough, strong enough, deserving enough ... we experience a block in this process. The universe knows that you are good, smart, valuable, important, strong and deserving – but it needs you to believe it too.

Unworthiness is kryptonite to co-creation. When we have feelings of low self-worth or inadequacy we are sending a strong message to the universe that we don't deserve the things we are trying to call in. We essentially block ourselves from receiving the love, success or happiness we long for because we simply believe we do not deserve it.

There are many reasons why we may feel unworthy: how we were raised, trauma, rejection, failure, social and cultural pressures – these things can all impact our self-worth. We start to believe that we aren't good enough, that we are less than, broken and flawed. This happens because when we connect our self-worth to negative thought patterns, we convince ourselves that our life experiences are proof we are unworthy. This is, once again, confirmation bias: when we have negative beliefs about ourselves and our worth, we begin to see evidence of our unworthiness everywhere we look. If we find ourselves here it can be challenging to change this direction and pull ourselves out of a cycle of low self-worth.

Unworthiness is sneaky. It can show up in many surprising ways and find its way into our psyche with ease. But sometimes unworthiness, doubt and worry are part of the tests that we can experience when we are deep in co-creating.

Imposter syndrome is a very specific type of unworthiness that can rear its head when we are co-creating. It's a phenomenon that causes a person to feel like a fraud because they don't believe they are deserving of what they have achieved. They believe they're not as capable as others perceive them to be and fear that they will be unmasked as imposters. This 'Who do I think I am?' thought pattern often feels like unreadiness, or a feeling that we must wait for someone else to give us permission to say 'yes' to the opportunity, desire or experience that we want.

This is not the energy we want when co-creating! We want – actually we *need* – to feel the exact opposite of imposter syndrome. We need to own our achievements and feel confident that we are exactly the kind of person who deserves everything they want. Instead of 'Why me?' shift your mindset to: 'Why *not* me?!'

Imposter syndrome can show up early on in your co-creation process; often at the asking phase, when we hear that voice of doubt creep in. But it can also happen when we have received what we have asked for – when the co-creation has *worked* – because it contradicts the evidence of our unworthiness that we've been gathering for so long. So, our brains need some re-wiring if we're going to get around this block. And, as with any limiting belief or thought-pattern, the first step is to simply notice it.

When it comes to imposter syndrome, our battle is with the voice that says, 'Who do you think you are?' or, 'How dare you ask for that?' I have found it helpful to give this voice a name. I use 'Negative Nancy', but we can call her Nancy for short.

When Nancy asks me, for example, 'Who do you think you are, to write a book about co-creation?' I stop, I pay attention, I acknowledge that Nancy is saying what she's been taught to say, and I respond, 'Hey, Nancy, I don't think like this anymore. I'm well-prepared, experienced, ready and capable to bring this information to the people who need it. I'm going to write a great book, and it's going to be a gift to those who receive it.' Instead of getting mad at Nancy, I simply update her understanding. Our Negative Nancys may resist us or need to be reminded often that we are no longer receptive to the imposter-syndrome talk. But eventually, if we engage lovingly with Nancy, she will get the message. And instead of telling us we're not ready, not good enough, not worth it, Nancy will fade out and make room for Positive Penny, who will be our cheerleader, encourage us and celebrate our wins.

To recap: we can combat imposter syndrome by noticing these imposter thoughts, reframing those thoughts, setting realistic goals and taking aligned action. Pride lists also work really well to remind us of our growing self-worth through our achievements and keep us in a healthy mindset. When we are really engaged in this process, our body will let us know: it will feel good, with a tingle of excitement, and a deep sense of calm that comes when we know we are right where we should be, and that everything ALWAYS works out for us.

I have had my own battles with imposter syndrome, and one of them still stands out for me to this day. A year or two after I had been hosting my very first TV show – which was a music video show – I was ready for something else. So, my agent got me a meeting with Channel 7 to explore the opportunity to join *The Morning Show* as a weekly contributor. This would involve panel discussions with feelgood news stories on fashion or pop culture. It was decided that I was going in to test with one of the hosts, just to see how the banter and the energy was. It was, in essence, a vibe check.

I was so excited that I now had more experience under my belt, and I felt ready for this new opportunity. I had built up my internal evidence in my previous role that proved I could do this, and I could already visualise it. And I did – I visualised every detail and primed my nervous system and body: imagining how relaxed, happy and connected I felt to everybody. So when I arrived, I felt like I was overflowing with joy, I was a ray of sunshine. I connected to everyone from the moment I drove into that parking lot and met the parking supervisor. I connected with the receptionist, the runner, the sound guy, the assistant, the hair and makeup team . . . everyone. And I went in there and didn't feel any nerves because I had primed myself so well that I already knew what everything would feel like.

I sat down across from David Campbell, who is still currently the host of that show. I was a little overwhelmed by the whole experience. Still, I felt centred and confident and sure that I'd done a great job. I went home and really trusted the process, satisfied that whatever happened now was meant to be. I had done the best job possible. Later, my agent called and said that they'd loved me . . . but, instead of the panellist role that I'd gone in for, would I consider auditioning for a hosting role which had just opened up? The imposter syndrome was *strong*. The hosts were in their late forties. I was only thirty, and I thought the role needed more wisdom and gravitas than I had. Who was

I to think I could just go in there and host *The Morning Show*? A national TV show. Surely there were more talented people that deserved this role who were already in the network. I thought, 'Okay, that's nice, but it can't be real.' And I realised that I didn't feel ready to host a whole show. This was a huge quantum leap. But I recognised that imposter syndrome had its hooks in me and I knew the only way to fight it was to do the *work*.

And so I did. I used all of my tools. I knew I needed to take aligned action. I began by asking for some feedback. They said to go take some autocue lessons. I booked them and I paid for them. (They were really expensive.) I started to do all the visualising and priming work again. Imagining myself sitting in hair and makeup at 4 am, driving there every day, parking, building relationships with the whole crew – putting the whole system in place. It was all working. When imposter syndrome popped up with unhelpful thoughts, I would say, 'Thank you, but I got this,' and, 'If it is meant for me, it will find me.' I kept priming my nervous system, kept practising, and then I went in for my audition.

I remember sitting waiting for my turn, and there was this incredible TV host called Sylvia Jeffreys there who was already on the network and is still there today. And I said to myself, 'There's no way you're going to get this. You're sitting next to Sylvia Jeffreys and she's way more experienced and she's already in the network . . .' It was imposter syndrome again. And again, I told it: 'I've got this.' I love Sylvia, she's a bloody rockstar, but I went in there and I was on fire. I was quick-witted, I was funny, I was sharp. I was a pro with that autocue – those expensive lessons paid off. I had arrived.

I connected more deeply with David that day. He said, 'You know, I think you're really great.'

And I got the job.

I got the job that made no sense for me – a thirty-year-old with very little experience on TV. I was going to host one of the biggest morning shows in the country. I could have let imposter syndrome win, and if I hadn't come back to the work – the work of co-creation – it would have.

The Abyss

The biggest way the universe tests us is with time. When you have called in your manifestation, your mindset is feeling powerful and supported, you've taken aligned action, removed blocks and you know you are deserving . . . and then? Nothing. You've done all the work and now you're waiting. And waiting. And waiting.

This is 'the Abyss'. It is the time between the calling in and the receiving. We all want this time to be as short as possible. We are ready, we've done all of the work. We have done our part in the co-creation partnership – so why the wait?

The universe is waiting to co-create with you to transform your wants into reality. But the calendar is a human invention, and the universe doesn't have a concept of time, nor does it operate according to our human ideas about what order things should happen in. It doesn't differentiate between what's happening 'now' and what's happening in 'the future'.

Personally, I find the Abyss to be the hardest part of this entire process. It's deeply uncomfortable for impatient people like me. It can make us question the whole process; it's frustrating and sometimes creates feelings of hopelessness, and this is even more pronounced for those of us who are new to co-creation. It can reignite the fires of doubt we have only just learned to put out.

If tests – those decoy manifestations that aren't quite good enough – are meant to challenge the clarity of our desires and our worthiness to receive them, the Abyss is here to test our trust in the process as a whole.

Trust is the key to making sure our manifestations arrive. Sitting in the Abyss is teaching you to trust the timing. 'Trust the timing' is the unofficial mantra of the Abyss. But it's confusing when you have been learning that the universe is always working for your greater good, and then you find yourself in the Abyss and it feels like nothing is happening, nothing is changing. Did your manifestation lose its way? Did the universe accidentally send your manifestation to someone else? No. The universe is teaching you that it doesn't operate on the same timeline as you do. It is saying: *Trust me, what is for you will never pass you by. You've asked, you shall receive. Just trust.*

I want to share a story about a time when I was well and truly in the Abyss – and how I got out of it. I've never shared this story before, but this feels like the right place. But before I go on, a little warning: I'm going to talk about fertility and pregnancy for the next couple of pages. I am well aware that this can be such an incredibly difficult and triggering topic for so many women, and the last thing I want this book to do is cause anyone pain. So, if you aren't in the right headspace to read about this right now, please skip ahead to the next section.

The truth is, although I'm a mum of two today, there was a time when I wasn't sure I wanted children. Before I became a mother, I was selfish in the best possible way. And I think some of the trauma that I had experienced from losing my mum made me scared to love someone that much again, in case I lost them. I also have a phobia called emetophobia, which is essentially an extreme fear of vomit. And we know with pregnancy and kids, it's a hard situation to avoid. I truly believed I could go through life being child-free. There was so much I wanted to achieve in my career and I was desperate to constantly travel – and I could only see myself doing these things without being a mum.

When I met my incredible husband, I knew he wanted children. And something happened when I met somebody that I could trust, who I knew would turn up wholeheartedly and even lead me as a parent. So, I started to open myself up to it. And, after exploring this with him and our therapist, I found out that my endometriosis – a disease in which tissue similar to the lining of the uterus grows *outside* of the uterus, causing severe pain and excessive bleeding – may impact my ability to conceive (despite having had it treated twice with surgery). At this time, I did some testing on the quality of my eggs and how many I had. Benji did some similar tests, and everything on his side looked normal. We knew from the endometriosis that it would already be difficult, but it also turned out that the number of eggs I had was really low. So the pressure was on and we decided to start trying.

I still had a lot of fear around motherhood and pregnancy, a lot of blocks. I did not feel ready. At first, when I didn't fall pregnant, I was relieved. But over time, conversations got more serious. Then we began discussing IVF and I started to wonder whether my uncertainty about motherhood was creating a block. Or was it the quality of the eggs? Or was it my endometriosis? Or was it all three?

And then we had a real breakthrough in our relationship. We were having therapy together and working through some of these blocks, and I felt a shift. There had been a psychological breakthrough in a session, a deep understanding of what needed to be in place for me to feel supported and safe enough to have a child, and Benji was willing to do whatever was needed to support me. I knew I was finally ready. I really wanted this baby. We had just moved to Brisbane and it seemed like the perfect time.

There was a very serendipitous moment where I received an email from a controversial Chinese medicine practitioner who invited me into his clinic – having already tried herbs and acupuncture to fall pregnant I was adamantly against ever having those herbs again. I can still taste them while I write this. That taste will haunt me forever. But I *was* looking for an acupuncturist, and this man was a practitioner. So I went in, and he said to me: 'I am going to give you an opportunity. I will treat you and you will be pregnant by June.' This was in February. 'You will not need IVF,' he said, 'but you need to follow every single thing I say.' I told him I didn't want to take herbs, but he insisted. Help! He also told me I would need to fast, and it wasn't just a juice fast for a few days. It was a two-week fast on nothing but water and herbs. This was a massive challenge for me. I'm a passionate foodie, I am thinking about the next meal whilst I'm eating my current one. My weekends revolve around trying new restaurants or catching up with friends over a great meal. When I travelled to Europe I researched where to eat, not where to stay. I get upset if I waste a meal on sub-par food. I am obsessed with food in the best possible way. It is my happiness. So even skipping a snack is hard, let alone no food at all for two weeks – only sips of water, black tea and Chinese herbs. Does it sound like pure hell? It was.

But I knew that this was also a huge opportunity that the universe was presenting to me. So, after much deliberation I agreed, I went through the process of turning up at this clinic every single morning. Fasting, ingesting herbs, detoxing, having treatments every day for a couple of hours (acupuncture, painful, rigorous massage, moxibustion and reflexology – none of which was pleasant). The emotional and physical toll was debilitating, and because so many social connections revolve around food, I also felt very isolated having just moved to Brisbane only to be the weird new girl who can't eat anything at all. Just trying to make friends was impossible, being around food was torture and I felt like death.

I was too dizzy to drive to my appointments most days so had to Uber in, I even went deaf in my right ear for two days. I could only really lie down and watch the day pass by. We hadn't set up our internet yet, so no wifi or streaming services. It was like the universe was really testing me, limiting the distraction from my discomfort. Out of desperation, one night I begged Benji to let me have his already eaten lamb cutlet bone so I could lick off the remaining salt and flavour. I googled how I could break the fast without my doctor knowing. I even tried negotiating with him over text late at night. I became obsessed with eating a juicy, crisp apple; I would fantasise about it. I didn't do it. But it was madness. It was intense.

After the initial two-week fast, I was allowed to slowly begin eating again – although I was still on a very restricted diet for the months to come. My first meal (if you can call it that) was half a cucumber. My practitioner told me that it was very important to break the fast slowly and gently – any other way can have dire consequences. Over the next couple of weeks, the program allowed me to eat very light meals, like steamed fish and greens.

At this point of my fertility treatment, there had been so much pain and sacrifice in just the first six weeks of this program that

I truly wanted to quit. I wanted to self-sabotage, I wanted to give up. I was well and truly in the Abyss. I had set my intention on having a baby, I had taken aligned action by signing up for the fertility program, and yet here I was – alone, depressed, starving and still not pregnant.

And when I was in the real depths of this process, feeling the challenge and the hardship, my best friend called me and told me she was pregnant. And I remember being so confronted by my own feelings. I was so happy for her, but (and this feels so shameful to share) I was also envious, not that she was pregnant but that it was easy for her. Up until now, she had been drinking alcohol and partying and having late nights and eating all the food she wanted. She had just been up to visit me in Brisbane and was living her best life, she hadn't had to give up the things I had given up . . . it seemed so effortless for her. She decided she wanted a baby and then she was pregnant. Why was my path to pregnancy so vastly different?

I couldn't even find the language to have this conversation with her because it was such a pure and exciting time and I didn't want to make it about me. And my heart truly goes out to all the other people who have faced fertility struggles. I realised the enormity of going on this journey, how painful trying to become a parent could be, how impossible and how heartbreaking it could feel.

And then I remembered how much love and opportunity I have in my life. This reminded me that I had my co-creation practice, and it hit me: my pregnant friend was a riiser for me at this moment in my life. Because another way to see a riiser is as proof that what you want is achievable. And she was showing me what was possible – I just needed to find my own way.

So I focused on my healing process. I moved into true surrender and accepted that if it was meant to be, I would have a baby. If that was my story and my journey, it would happen. And if the program I was attempting didn't work, then we would find another way – we would start IVF at the end of the year. And if IVF didn't work, there were still other avenues to explore to grow our family, and I was going to have to be okay with that. All I could do was trust that whether it was my body or someone else's that carried my baby, I would get through this time in the Abyss – one way or another.

This surrender and trust released some of the pressure I was feeling, it helped me relax and feel more hopeful at a time when I was utterly hopeless (and did I mention hungry?). I decided to really trust that what was for me would find me, and instead of anxiously worrying about why I wasn't pregnant yet and what the future would hold, I focused on being present and grateful, and completing the program I had committed to.

As we reached winter the doctor's words echoed in my mind. *Pregnant by June*. And then it happened. The morning of my 33rd birthday, bleary eyed and half asleep I took a pregnancy test without thinking anything other than it being a green light that I could have a couple drinks to celebrate at my birthday that night. Gob smacked and shaking I went to Benji at 6 am holding the stick, falling to the ground sobbing.

I want to pause here and say that I wasn't sure I'd share this story in these pages, because fertility journeys, pregnancy and childbirth are all such complicated and nuanced things. And there was also always the very real possibility that I might not have fallen pregnant – even after the fertility program, even with the help of IVF. I don't believe that I manifested my pregnancy. But I absolutely do believe that the steps I took helped me get through this challenging time. Setting my intention, taking aligned action with the fertility program, making my pregnant friend a riiser rather than a rival, and then surrendering to the Abyss – all of these steps supported me in one way or another, and made this difficult period more bearable.

The reason that I chose to share this story is because it teaches us not only that the Abyss is part of the process, but also introduces the idea of a 'divine redirect' – in other words, what can happen when what we ask for doesn't appear in the way we'd hoped. Like most women who want to have a baby, I had hoped to get pregnant without help, and certainly without having to fast for weeks. But that wasn't how it happened for me. There were times when I felt doubt, worry, and even envy about my friend's easy pregnancy. My experience is that by accepting the alternative treatment and taking significant aligned action in this process, as well as by educating myself about the impacts of my endometriosis and egg count, I ultimately got to a place where I was able to sit in deep trust that what was meant for me would be.

Ultimately, I received the news I wanted, and I am so grateful for that. But it might not have gone this way. And I had to make peace with the idea that if it wasn't going to happen for me, I would find other ways to have a family; opportunities to foster or adopt. I was aware that there may be a divine redirect in store for me, and I accepted that.

When we are in the Abyss, it's always a possibility that what we believe we want may not match what the universe knows we need. Just as we are tested with those decoy manifestations that give us the opportunity to say, 'Nope, not quite right,' sometimes the universe may decide that what we have asked for is not for our greater good, no matter how desperately we want it. Remember, we think we know what's best for us, but this isn't always true. It can be infuriating and uncomfortable, not getting what you want when you want it. So, we have to get comfortable with the unknown, a paradoxical balance between learning to co-create and also trusting that the universe, or our higher power knows what's best for us.

As I've already shared, I had always wanted to be an actor. I was inspired by Meryl Streep and wanted to tell stories on screen. I wanted it so badly, I asked for it time and again. And I did receive opportunities occasionally, but no matter how hard I tried it wasn't for me. I won't lie, I experienced pain and frustration with the constant disappointment. Not getting what you want sucks.

The universe didn't ignore what I wanted, it just appeared in a different way. It looked different to how I expected it would. From 'not making it' as an actress, I ended up getting the opportunity with a music show. I wasn't playing a major role on the big screen – actually, I wasn't playing a role at all. I was just being me. It was much more authentic. And I realised that was what I really needed: it was *better* than what I had asked for. I would never have been able to be myself as a character actor. And authenticity was what my soul truly yearned for. This little music show launched my TV and radio career, which led me to my internationally award-winning podcast *The Deep*, and ultimately to you, right now – sharing my story and teaching you the process of co-creation in this book.

If it sounds like I'm asking you to hold more than one truth at a time, I am. If it sounds like I'm telling you to ask clearly for what you want, to believe and expect it to manifest, while at the same time maintaining grace and trust to recognise that sometimes what we truly need may be different to what we *thought* we wanted . . . I am. And the link between these seemingly unrelated elements is your intuition, your deepest inner knowing. A test will never feel right in the way that a divine redirect feels right. And I promise, the more you learn to listen to your intuition, the more you are able to find the balance between what you want and what the universe knows, the easier it will get. The tests will be less frequent, and your time in the Abyss will be shorter.

MEDITATION FOR JOURNEYING THROUGH THE ABYSS

This meditation is designed to support you when you find yourself in the Abyss. We know the Abyss is the time in between calling in what we want and it manifesting in our lives. We've done all of the work, taken the aligned action, healed our blocks, let go, trusted, surrendered, and then we land in the Abyss. But once you've been in the Abyss you know that it is an integral part of the manifestation process and there is no way of avoiding this. Of course, some manifestations come immediately while with others you may find yourself in the Abyss perhaps for weeks or even months. The Abyss requires us to have deep trust and unwavering faith that what is meant for us will find us. It requires us to surrender. This short, guided meditation is intended to help you through this time.

First, make yourself comfortable somewhere private, where you're alone and will not be distracted or interrupted. Sometimes when we're in the Abyss we can feel contracted and tight throughout the chest, throat and stomach, so if you're lying down I want you to spread your arms wide open. If you're seated, roll your shoulders back, hold your arms out slightly to the side, relaxed, palms up.

Take five deep breaths, holding them for a beat before breathing out. Start to notice where you're holding tension in your body. What needs to be released? If you are in the Abyss I'm almost certain there are feelings of unease. So using your breath to anchor you, breath in and begin to release some of that tension. The purpose of this meditation is to acknowledge this feeling and breathe through it so it has less power over you and your nervous system.

Breathe in trust, knowing you're exactly where you're meant to be even if you are uncomfortable, breathe out and release anxiety, knowing that it's normal for the human mind to want to be in control.

Breathe in *ultimate* trust and surrender, imagining a beautiful white light above you. As the light slowly envelops you, breathe out any desperation, restrictions, deadlines or anything in your mind and body that is holding you back.

This white light is the universe holding you, supporting you, letting you know that it has got you and you don't need to do anything but let go and trust it.

The white light feels beautiful and supportive, warm as it flows through your body, from the feet to the top of the head where it reminds you to breathe out and let go of control.

Breathe in and take a beat here, feel into the knowing that the universe has your back – that the universe is working for your greater good, and that the more you sink into trust the more space you are giving it to work out what you truly need.

Breathe out all that control, anxiety, doubt and worry.

Sit with your breathing for a moment and acknowledge that, as you find yourself in the Abyss, this is a temporary state. Just like everything in life. Nothing good or bad lasts forever. With every breath in, you are manifesting the life you deserve. And with every breath out, you are letting go of your impatience and frustration as you allow yourself to fall deeper into trusting in the universe.

Instead of fighting the Abyss, accept that this time is expected and necessary. Understand that you never know what's happening behind the scenes. This is your time to wait patiently. Breathe in and know that this part of the process is simply testing how much you trust it. Breathe out and release any expectation or frustration, knowing that you are exactly where you're supposed to be.

As you start to wiggle your fingers and toes and make your way back to the room, know that you are divinely held, and that the white light is inside you always. You are safe and a true magnet for the life you deserve.

Sacrifice

If you've drifted away from a friendship that didn't feel right anymore, or if you've ever had a break-up with a partner or decided to quit a job, then you've experienced the feeling of outgrowing a relationship or situation that no longer matches the person you have become. While these are natural ebbs and flows that all of us experience, it doesn't make it easier when these moments are upon us.

The deeper your connection to yourself, the universe, and co-creation becomes, the clearer it will become which relationships and situations no longer serve you. As you live your truth, you'll become aware when certain relationships and circumstances conflict with that truth. The more true you are to yourself, the more intolerable you will find relationships and situations that don't align with you. As you create new habits and beliefs, it becomes harder to maintain relationships and situations that pull you back toward ones that you have outgrown, or that never served you in the first place.

Because of all this, manifesting the life we desire often requires sacrifice. We tend to have a strong reaction to the word sacrifice. Often we associate it with deprivation, loss, powerlessness or tragedy. And while there are certainly times where sacrifice can be painful, for our purposes it refers to the necessity of making space in our lives for what we are co-creating and that which we truly deserve.

Think about it like this: your couch is falling apart, it's dirty, the springs are poking through and it dips when you sit down. You know that you need a new one. So, you save up and buy a beautiful new couch. But when it arrives . . . the old one is still there, sitting in your lounge room. And suddenly all the happy memories you made on that couch come back to you: eating popcorn with your kids, kissing your partner, talking late into the night with friends. It feels absolutely impossible, in that moment, to let go: to make the sacrifice. But you can't fit that big, beautiful new couch in your lounge room if you don't get rid of the old one. You have to trust that you will make new memories – that good things will come even though it's painful to let go of familiar comforts.

Sacrifice can be difficult, but it's essential to make room in your life for the good things you deserve. If you would like to manifest a job where you feel stimulated and valued, you may need to leave the one that is currently paying the bills – and the comfort of doing something familiar. If you would like to manifest a relationship where you feel supported and loved, you may need to leave the one that makes you feel isolated and taken for granted – even at the cost of feeling alone for some time in between. If you want to manifest more courage, you might have to sacrifice some of the comfort of playing it safe. In this sense, sacrifice is more like a shedding of an old skin that no longer fits us. Still uncomfortable, but necessary.

It's important we also shed those parts of ourselves that no longer match the vibration we are now aligned with. This can be uncomfortable. It can involve a kind of grief for those parts of ourselves that no longer serve us, even if they are comforting to us. But the reward is living a life that aligns with our truest self, a life that we are proud of.

When you are living as the highest version of yourself, everything changes. You will move differently, speak differently, think differently. You will hold yourself in a place of worthiness and value, and when you have moved through your blocks, you will begin to treat yourself differently. You will expect more of yourself, and of the people you choose to allow into your life. You won't tolerate anything less. Momentary comforts like being around toxic friends so you're not alone, or binge drinking to numb your feelings, or even overworking to prove your worth – all of these things will begin to feel strangely out of place when you decide to live in your truth. You will soon realise that these 'comforting' or 'pleasurable' habits aren't compatible with the life you want to live – even though they may have been a big part of your life prior to evolving.

Once you've come to this understanding, you won't be able to pretend you don't know what you're doing. Ignorance is bliss, but you no longer have the blinkers on. You're no longer just responding to external stimuli over which you have no control. Because now you know better, and you have chosen this path. And this path, the one that leads to the life you deserve, requires discipline and sacrifice. What is that saying body builders and athletes love? 'No pain, no gain!'

Boundaries

The boundaries you set with other people aren't for them; they are for you. Boundaries are essential for healthy relationships, but, more than anything else, they protect *you*. Boundaries are kind of like the door bitch outside a nightclub – if the nightclub is your soul, your energy and your nervous system, then boundaries are the tough-looking bouncer at the door deciding who is allowed to enter (and who gets kicked out!). Your club is exclusive, private and elite. You can't just let in any old riff raff off the street.

But what happens if your bouncer is a pushover? Suddenly the club wouldn't be so exclusive anymore; you'd have drunk people peeing on the walls, smashing glasses, starting fights with one another – it would be awful! And the club – your soul – would be at serious risk of damage. Boundaries are there to make sure that this doesn't happen. That stunning, invite-only, state of the art club that is your soul should stay that way: exclusive, beautiful, peaceful.

I have many boundaries. The more of this work I teach and practice the more I put in place. To me, boundaries feel good and powerful. They feel clear. When I meet someone who has strong boundaries, it tells me they know themselves, respect themselves, love themselves.

If you haven't had great boundaries so far (like so many people pleasers) then they can feel very awkward and uncomfortable in the beginning. It can even feel like we're being mean or rude, especially when other people aren't used to us setting them.

Why are boundaries so important for co-creation? It's because our energy can be influenced by other people. Nobody can manifest for us, and we can't manifest for others, but what we *can* do is influence each other's state of mind and energy. You know what it's like when you enter a room at the worst possible moment, right after a huge argument or an awkward pause in the conversation, and you can just feel the tension in the air? Energy is contagious and can impact us. In this context, boundaries operate on two levels: we need boundaries around who we share our co-creation journey with, and boundaries around those people and things in our lives that may take our precious attention away from it.

We must be careful about who we choose to speak to about our co-creation, because we want to talk to people who are going to add to the magic, who want for us what we want for ourselves, who delight in our success and growth. We don't want Negative Nancys around who will suck us right back into the thought-patterns and habits that we've worked so hard to change. You can feel it in your gut when someone isn't really celebrating with you. Trust that feeling, and avoid sharing co-creation with these people, all the way up until your manifestation has arrived. Then, let them see what you have achieved. You never know, you may even become one of their riisers, a source of great inspiration.

We also need boundaries around the kind of people, environments and energy we expose ourselves to more generally. Something I pay very close attention to is how people make me feel when I'm around them. Do I leave their company feeling calm and inspired, understood and loved, respected and protected? Or do I leave their company feeling stressed and depleted, misunderstood and frustrated? Ask yourself: Do I have a friendship or relationship that has become co-dependent or disrespectful? This might look like a friend who only reaches out when they need you to help with their problems, or who is happy to trauma dump on you even when they know you're on an important deadline or spending time with your family. Whatever the case may be, it's time to really tune into how other people make you feel – what signs and messages your body is sending you about them – and slowly you will start to shift towards only spending time with people who fill your cup as much as you fill theirs.

At times, we may also need to put boundaries in place around work. I don't care how important you are or how much money you make, no one needs to be on call 24/7! And if you feel that your time is not being respected and you are being inundated with work-related requests at all hours, you may need to have a conversation and put some boundaries in place with your colleagues so they respect your personal time.

At first, it can be difficult to set boundaries. But if we want to have healthy boundaries, we can't avoid difficult moments or conversations – even if we suspect it may rock the boat, be uncomfortable or hurt someone's feelings. Establish your boundaries with clear and kind communication. Remind those that overstep your boundaries what they are and don't be afraid of upsetting them – you are doing what is fair and necessary for you to thrive.

It's also important to note that even the strongest boundaries can get crossed. This is completely normal. Simply re-establish them, kindly yet firmly, and take note of who has disrespected you and your peace so that they won't get past your boundaries next time.

Part 5

The Journey
Ahead

Have you ever heard of the Hero's Journey? It's a framework often used by storytellers that was made famous by Joseph Campbell, who was a professor of literature at Sarah Lawrence College. He argued that there was a common structure to the world's mythology, a structure called the Hero's Journey. The Hero's Journey has three stages:

1. The Departure: when the hero must leave his or her familiar world behind and venture forth into the unknown.
2. The Initiation: when the hero, through a series of challenges, learns he or she has the power within to succeed.
3. The Return: when the hero returns to his or her world, triumphant and forever changed.

You are the hero of your own life. You are the main character. You're reading this book because you were ready to depart on an adventure: to leave behind your old familiar ways of thinking and learn some new ones. You listened to your inner knowing, which connected you to this practice, and to a new relationship with yourself and the universe. And if you've come up against any of the tests and blocks we discussed in the previous chapter, then you have also experienced the 'Initiation' stage. But you still have one more part of this transformative journey to complete, and that is the 'Return'. This chapter is all about how you can maintain momentum in manifesting the life you deserve, move past the initiation stage, and make it back home as a master manifestor – powerful, triumphant and forever transformed.

Here, we will learn the principles that will help keep us on track to becoming audacious co-creators. You've learned so much, and I know you are well on your way, taking your time with whatever parts of this work need the most attention from you, and being gentle with yourself always. Now it's time to talk about co-creation as a lifestyle, and what you can do to integrate this work into your life and maintain momentum and motivation. But first, let's remember how we got here.

RECAP

1. You wanted to learn more about co-creation and you followed your intuition to this book, where you learned what co-creation is (and what it isn't).

2. You have set an intention for yourself: what it is you want to experience, manifest, learn and do as you co-create with the universe. Essentially, you have asked.

3. You took the time to think about what your core values and beliefs are, and how to bring your intentions into true alignment with this value system.

4. You have learned to catalogue your thoughts, becoming aware of the negative self-talk and limiting beliefs that don't support

co-creation, and how to replace them with pride in yourself and trust in the universe.

5. You've discovered how to attain neutral, and how important this is for the process of manifestation.

6. You have learned how to create a mindset of abundance and gratitude – the universe loves this.

7. You've found clarity about your co-creations by testing them against your core values, as well as by finding riisers who embody your hopes and aspirations.

8. You have filled your co-creation toolbox with techniques to strengthen your practice: from journalling, meditation, the Switch, affirmations, pride lists and visualisations, to taking aligned action, creating rituals to support your co-creation, and even rewriting the story of your life.

9. You have acknowledged that with this work you will encounter blocks and tests, and that you may find yourself in the Abyss – waiting and worrying. But you are strong in the knowledge that you are equipped with all the tools you need to get through whatever the universe throws at you. You sit in trust.

10. You have arrived here, ready and willing to continue with this work and maintain all the momentum that you have built up. And that is what this chapter is all about.

I mentioned at the beginning of this book that co-creation is a lifestyle. It's not a hobby or a moment in time. One of the reasons why I became so passionate about co-creation was that I saw the evidence of it show up in quantifiable ways in my life and the lives of others who were also mindfully manifesting. This is how I knew that it wasn't just woo-woo, or a quick-fix scheme.

And like anything valuable it requires practice, commitment and consistency.

So how do we integrate the co-creation mindset into our lives? How do we maintain momentum, even when things go wrong? In this final chapter, we're going to look at what we can do to support our co-creation practice as we continue on this journey, and especially when we feel we are lacking motivation or slipping back into old habits.

Maintaining Momentum

When we feel a lack of motivation, taking a step back can often be the best first move. Go back to basics and revisit the insights you've already discovered – the pages you dog-eared and the parts you highlighted. Think of it like watering already germinating seeds, ready to break through the soil. This is a chance to refresh your understanding and get excited. Don't let it overwhelm you, it's just like a quick refresher course of the points you need to remember.

What going 'back to basics' means in this context is different for each of us, but the first step is always to find neutral. Remember, neutral is the state required for us to co-create. It feels like balanced emotions (which doesn't mean you aren't experiencing *challenging* emotions, it just means that there is room for the light and the shade). Neutral feels like space and curiosity.

Once you're back in neutral, meditate on your mindset. The ultimate motivational and inspirational tool we have at our disposal is gratitude: real, genuine, authentic, feel-the-joy-permeate-your-body gratitude. We will have our bad days and days that blindside us ... but when we find one thing to be grateful for, no matter how simple or small, we are on our way back to alignment, to neutral, to our best selves, and to co-creation.

It's also important to revisit your beliefs and core values, and check that they are truly aligned with what you're trying to manifest. Has ego or judgement crept in along the way? Reassess your manifestations – don't just take it for granted that what you wanted a year ago is what you need now. We are always evolving and our manifestations are too.

Another way we can find motivation is through our riisers. As we have learned, riisers are people who already have what we want. When we were operating at a lower vibration, we might have felt envy towards them. But now, because we know better and align with a higher vibration, we are inspired and motivated by these people and their achievements. We have learned that these riisers are no different than us. If they can do it, so can we.

Our pride and gratitude lists are another invaluable resource when we're lacking motivation. Through these lists, we have banked evidence that we can refer to when we feel anxious or doubtful. When we fall into old patterns that may come back to test us, the evidence of what we have manifested before reminds us we can and will manifest again. And this is how we stay motivated.

Finally, let me remind you of the power of the Switch! Whether you're in a downward spiral or just feeling a little lost and uninspired, making the Switch and shifting your energy and vibe by using a simple circuit breaker to help you get there can supercharge you with the energy you need to get back on track with your co-creation.

Remember, even if we get into a slump with co-creation, the universe is always ready, always working for our greater good.

Acceptance and The Divine Redirect

When we recognise that we're being tested or that we are in the Abyss, we have two options: we can throw up our hands, have a tantrum, and give up (which will lead us back to our comfort zone), or we can acknowledge that all transformation requires us to face ourselves, to sit in the discomfort of the patterns that need to change, and, ultimately, to trust.

I'm going to let you in on a little secret about co-creation and manifestation: it's not about *things*. That is not to say that we are not learning how to co-create some things that we want: more money, a dream job, a nice house, a soulmate. However, the real gift of co-creation is the peace, happiness and deep contentment that arrives when we know beyond a shadow of a doubt that the universe has our back, and that everything always works out for us.

Acceptance works on two levels in co-creation. First, we learn to *accept* that the universe is guiding us towards what we truly require to live authentically – even if sometimes it takes a while for our manifestations to appear. Then, we *accept* the rewards of our co-creation. In this sense, acceptance involves both letting go of our resistance to the universe's flow and receiving what it sends our way. We all know how great it feels to accept something we have asked for. But the other kind of acceptance – acknowledging that the universe knows what it's doing – is much harder to wrap our heads around.

This can be a challenging concept for newcomers to co-creation because acceptance can feel like the opposite of co-creation. Aren't we supposed to be specific about what we want? Doesn't the universe like specificity and focused attention? Yes. But we must also trust that the universe may take us down a path we didn't ask for, or present us with a manifestation that looks different to what we requested, and that sometimes the universe may actually *decline* to co-create certain things with us.

This is a hard one to swallow. Sometimes we think we know exactly what we want. We are adamant *that* thing is *the* thing. But then it doesn't happen and we are left wondering what went wrong – where *we* went wrong. We start to ask ourselves questions like 'What could I have done differently?' or 'Did I not want it enough?' or even 'What the actual *%$#?'.

What we perceive as a rejection or as the co-creation process not working is most often something referred to as 'divine redirection'. I describe divine redirection as the universe changing course in order to reach the best outcome for our higher selves in the long term. But this can also feel disappointing or disheartening. You will be confused about why that guy didn't call back or why you didn't get the job. And only after weeks or months, when the universe has presented what was REALLY best for you (the divine redirect), will you understand that there was a greater purpose at play.

I've had many painful divine redirections. I've already shared with you how my dreams of being an actor ultimately led me into radio and to where I am now. But here's another one that really hurt: I had just landed that incredible job, hosting *The Morning Show*. I was in the door, they loved me. At this time, I had a deep awareness that this was the opportunity that signalled the beginning of my TV career. It was such a big, visible role, and I knew that this was my moment. It was, however, a short-term role – I would be filling in for the regular host while they were away on a different project. But this is what was so exciting to me – it was the perfect platform, and the idea of what might come next was thrilling.

And then, out of nowhere, my husband sits me down and says, 'I'm really unhappy with where I'm at in my career. I want to take a chance. I want to change from rugby league to rugby union over in New Zealand. What do you think?' And I was just floored. I told him that I wanted him to be happy, to feel purpose-ful, but I'd only just got my foot in the door with this new role. He explained that he'd been offered a really big opportunity in rugby union, but we'd have to move to New Zealand immediately. I felt like I'd been punched in the gut. 'Shit,' I thought, 'I just got a job with a major network, and if I leave now, will they ever let me back in?' My career dreams were coming true. But in Benji's world, everything had lined up for him, too. So what were we going to do? I knew I had to be with him. I wanted to be with him. We had only just got married. And so, I grounded myself, I meditated and focused on gratitude, and I trusted that this was a divine redirect.

I told the network and my new colleagues that I needed to go with Benji to New Zealand – they were disappointed, and so was I, but at the end of the day they supported my decision. We moved to New Zealand the following week.

It was scary, I wasn't sure what was going to be there for me. I didn't know anybody. It was going to be a whole new life for maybe a year, maybe five years, depending on how it went. But Benji was a superstar – New Zealand is his home, his culture. There was so much buzz and excitement, all of these newspaper articles about him – everyone was so pumped.

And, to my surprise, as soon as I landed in New Zealand people began throwing work opportunities at me: a prime time afternoon radio show, TV show offer after TV show offer. It turned out that this divine redirect gave me some of the biggest opportunities that I've ever had. I hosted a travel TV show called *The Great Food Race* with the very well-known and respected producer, Julie Christie. And as we travelled all around New Zealand and even to China for the show, I was really able to hone my skills and my craft under her guidance very quickly. It was such an incredible adventure. Lots of learning, lots of hard times, but it got me to where I needed to be.

I also accepted a role with a prime time national radio show, and it was the most fun I'd had at work. I realised that *this* was what I really wanted to do. After that, I moved away from TV and into radio. But if I hadn't gone to New Zealand, I might never have discovered that radio was my thing. The devastation I felt from losing the opportunity with *The Morning Show* faded, because the sacrifice had opened up this huge, infinite possibility. And at the time, flying into the unknown of New Zealand, I had no idea what was around the corner for me. I just had to lean in and trust, and marvel at what I had co-created.

It doesn't feel good to be on the receiving end of a universal 'no' – particularly if we have followed all of the steps and done all of the work required for successful co-creation. We can start to spiral into negativity and some of the blocks we have learned about – doubt, worry and unworthiness – begin to creep in.

When you are presented with a 'no', always remember that you have a choice. If you choose to slip into a negative thought loop and start obsessing about getting *that* thing and only that thing, then you risk missing out on what is actually on its way to you. If you choose to stay open, fall deeper into your motivations for wanting that thing in the first place, and trust the co-creation process, then you open yourself up to accepting a divine redirect. And who knows where it might take you?

Simply put, a divine redirect occurs when you don't get what you want because something else, something bigger, brighter and more aligned to your truth, is on its way to you. A phrase that embodies this principle is: *rejection is redirection.* It is rooted in the old adage, 'when one door closes, another opens'.

This is why we spend so much time focusing on our core values, our belief systems and thought patterns. It's all about connecting with the essence of what we are seeking and not just the *thing* that we desire. When we say we want more money, aren't we really saying that we want more peace and less stress, more opportunity and freedom? When we say we want a soulmate, aren't we really saying that we want authentic connection and a sense of belonging? When we say we want a new house, are we not saying that we want stability and safety and comfort? When we say we want a new job, are we not saying that we want to be appreciated and stimulated and validated in our work? When we can really lean into the *why* and not get overly caught up in the *what*, we can move through these divine redirections more easily.

One of the strongest lessons I've learned about acceptance is how to surrender to these divine redirections in life. It's just like that old saying: 'Let go or be dragged.'

This is not a story about 'giving up' when things get too hard or don't go the way you want. This is a story of choosing to trust yourself and the universal signs showing you the way. We have to *trust* and *accept* that when a 'no' happens it's because there is something better around the corner.

FYI

There have been so many scientific advancements that have illuminated how our brains operate, and what powerful engines they really are. EEG or electroencephalogram technology measures the different kinds of brain waves or signals that our brains emit when we are doing various activities. There are five primary brain waves, which are, in essence, frequencies that our brain's internal electrical systems operate with:

- Beta: This is our external attention frequency, often linked to anxiety, when we are focused on outside influences that we may perceive as threats.
- Gamma: This is associated with deep focus and concentration.
- Theta: These wavelengths are about deep relaxation and inward focus – this is the frequency we hope for during meditation.
- Delta: This is the deep sleep frequency.

But it's the 'Alpha' frequency that I want to tell you about now. Alpha brain waves are connected to relaxation and passive attention – our brains might be operating in an alpha state when we are just waking up or falling asleep, when we are listening to music in the background. Alpha waves are about a kind of quiet, passive attention. Neuroscientists have also shown that we are at our most creative when we're in an alpha state.[13] Alpha brain waves can be thought of as supporting a state of flow.

A lot of the work that we do in co-creation – from visualisation to priming, journaling and gratitude practices, rituals and routines – have great benefits when practised in an alpha state.

---

13 Andreas Fink and Mathias Benedek, 'EEG alpha power and creative ideation' *Neuroscience and Biobehavioral Reviews* 44(100) (2014), at pp 111–123.

Trust the Process

In the modern world that we live in, we are told that becoming a successful adult is about having control over ourselves, our lives and circumstances. We are also told that we should be wary of people or institutions that seek to take our control away, or who use their control to manipulate us. I've already shared my personal story with you about my experience of an extremley unsafe relationship that was violent and based in coercive control. I am very wary of giving up my control. Because for me – and likely for many of you – giving up control is unsafe. It feels like giving up our power, agency and rights.

I'm not asking you to set aside your relationship to control when it comes to people or the systems and frameworks of society. Instead, I am asking you to focus on your relationship with control when it comes to the universe, your partner in co-creation. There is an inherent power imbalance between the universe and us. The universe is a highly intelligent creator. After all, the universe – or God, or higher power – created itself, the cosmos, the galaxies, our earth and us. The universe is not something anyone can dictate to, and thinking of it this way will only lead to frustration.

Surrendering can be one of the trickiest parts of co-creation because most of us think we know what's best for us. We think that our plan and our strategy is the exact thing that will get us what we want and if we do everything 'right', it will happen for us. But we must remember that co-creation is *collaboration*. When we try to manipulate or control the variables, we aren't in aligned action, trust and collaboration – we are in a desperate state, trying to dominate the system rather than work with it.

Co-creation can feel like throwing yourself a birthday party. You've sent out the invites. You've organised the cake, the decorations, the flowers and the music. Then you have to wait. You have to sit in your living room in your party dress waiting for all your friends to arrive. You have to trust that all the careful planning and organising is going to pay off. If the first guest is late to arrive then you can start to spiral, thinking that no one is going to show up – we've all been there. But you can't call each guest and ask them if they're on their way. You have to *trust* that you are loved and will be supported. And before you know it, people begin to arrive. You just have to *accept* that if there are certain people on your invite list who can't make it, there is likely a harmless reason that is not personal.

And, like the birthday party, co-creation can make us feel vulnerable because we don't have control. However, it's super important to know when to let go and trust. It can be hard. It can be scary. But, like any practice, the more we work to trust and accept – and the more evidence we gather that trust and acceptance work – the easier it becomes to continue to trust and accept in the future.

I want to share a story about trust and control. As I've mentioned earlier, there's a phobia I've been challenged by my whole life, called emetophobia: the fear of vomiting. It's a strange thing – no one *likes* vomiting, diarrhoea, pus, blood, or any of those things, but few of us are actually consumed by the thought of them. It all started when I was around nine years old. I caught some kind of virus and vomited so many times I ended up throwing up blood. I lost control over all my bodily functions, and my mum wasn't there at the time to help me. I was so scared and full of shame.

Ariise

By the time I was a teenager, my fear of vomiting had turned into an obsession. In fact, I was living with Obsessive Compulsive Disorder. I was so afraid of getting sick that I wouldn't eat out, and I started washing my hands until they were cracked and bleeding. I even wore a scarf around my mouth and nose like a mask at school to avoid getting sick. It was something that impacted my day-to-day life for so many years.

As an adult, after many attempts at therapy and hypnotism, I decided that I needed to go somewhere that specialised in my condition. I started a program based in the UK where they give you a couple of tests to determine the cause of the phobia. And one of these tests is checking whether you rely predominantly on your internal or external 'locus of control'. Do you rely primarily on yourself – your internal sense of control – to get through hard times, or do you rely on other people, spirituality, manifestation, God, or religion – in other words, things that are outside of yourself?

I understood the purpose of the test and what the therapist was getting at: it can be beneficial for us to have a strong internal locus of control, so that when we are faced with adversity or a phobia – in my case, vomiting – we know that no matter what happens, we can handle it.

My program therapist and I got to a really tricky place. He knew I was dedicated to co-creating and manifesting, and he asked me if I was willing to suspend that for a few weeks to see if we could explore the possibility that everything in my life was of my *own* creation – no universe, no higher power involved. My phobia therapist was asking me to put all of my core beliefs around co-creation into a kind of suspension.

'I want you to live practically,' he said, 'scientifically, and use your *internal* locus of control.' I was so committed to this program that I decided to try it, and it really did challenge and surprise me.

Through this lens, when I looked around at this home that I had manifested, and my career and my achievements ... I thought, '*Holy shit*, did I just do all of that myself?' I felt really proud of myself and in that moment I understood the process and the lesson of the program. But, after a few weeks of truly engaging with the idea that I am the only entity that is in control of me, I knew something was off.

So, I went back to my therapist and I told him that I could see the power in what he was teaching. He didn't want me to hit a moment of fear – of vomiting or anything else – and barter with a higher power to get through it. He wanted me to know that I have the tools to deal with whatever comes. There was great value in this lesson and I didn't disregard it, but I had to be honest with him. I explained to him that without my relationship to the universe, life didn't feel as rich or colourful or exciting. It didn't feel as deep, it didn't feel as mysterious, and there was no sense of infinite opportunity. Life suddenly had limits.

He understood this completely and encouraged me to carry forward what I'd learned into my relationship to co-creation and manifestation. 'But,' he explained, 'also know that the power is in you.' I told him what I shared with you at the beginning of this book, that this is precisely why I prefer the term co-creation to manifestation. I do have a strong sense of my internal locus of control, but I'm also working with a higher power to support me. I'm trusting in that higher power and relinquishing *some* of my control – not all of it.

And, if shit hits the fan and my phobia rears its ugly head, co-creating and trusting in the universe helps me to get through that. Yes, I am in the driver's seat, I'm doing the work, but I'm anchored in my faith and the support system of the universe.

Patience

Modern human beings are not great at waiting. I AM THE WORST. Our waiting muscle has atrophied as technology and systems have advanced that are based on speed, immediacy and instant gratification. Drive-thru fast food, same-day deliveries, immediate responses to our questions online. If we want to talk to someone on the other side of the globe, we simply call them. Not that long ago we would have had to wait weeks for letters to be delivered by ships.

Have I experienced great speed with the co-creation process? Yes, from time to time, I have witnessed a quick turnaround. Especially with micro-manifesting. But, more often than not, there is a time frame which we must ... trust! Trusting the timing is a very important part of co-creation. Co-creation needs time. Co-creation needs patience.

Even after all these years of working with co-creation, sometimes I can turn into a demanding little child. Especially when my desire is strong and I feel ready for whatever it is I'm asking for. Or if there is a sense of urgency on my end – maybe a deadline that I am trying to meet, and I want the universe to work with my timeframe. At times, I am the most impatient and unrealistic person I know. This is part of my nature and will be a work in progress. And even though I have not perfected this part of myself, co-creation still works for me abundantly and dependably, every time.

Celebrate Your Wins

In Australia we have a concept called 'Tall Poppy Syndrome'. Basically, it's a form of success shaming. It implies that the poppy flower that grows too tall – or a person that becomes too successful – is going attract attention, and must be cut down. No one is allowed to shine too bright. What we're meant to learn from this metaphor is that we shouldn't be too loud about our success, we shouldn't celebrate or be too showy about our achievements. This is especially true for women – we avoid celebrating ourselves altogether, for fear of being called arrogant or conceited.

In my travels, I've observed that it's the complete opposite for many Americans – they are all about championing success, they want to see it loud and proud, splashed across billboards. People are inspired by the success of others, they lean in and are curious and less judgemental.

Perhaps we want to be somewhere in the middle; humility, especially when it comes to the universe, is essential. But we don't want to be humble to the point of making ourselves small, of being afraid to take up too much space in the world. We want to strive for what is sometimes referred to as 'Main Character Energy'. As you already know, you are the main character in your life.

Co-creation requires us to unlearn many old, outdated, unhelpful beliefs and habits, and belittling success is one of them. We must learn a little from our American friends and remain in awe of those who are making it big. We want to delight in our co-creations. When our manifestations arrive we must celebrate them. When we don't do this, it's as if someone we have missed for a very long time has travelled a great distance to visit us and yet, when they turn up on our doorstep, all we can manage is, 'Oh, it's you.' That's incredibly disappointing and disrespectful. So, when our manifestations arrive, we should greet them with excitement and delight and gratitude and joy.

Pride lists are one way of celebrating our manifestations – especially the smaller ones that can all too easily go unnoticed. It's highly recommended that you celebrate with big, excited energy when you manifest the big, exciting things. This doesn't mean bragging, or making other people feel small – although remember, you don't need to make yourself small to make other people feel better (you will become a riiser for them). A big celebration can be quiet and private – as long as the feeling is there, and you allow yourself that sense of achievement and pride.

The universe thrives on delight. Celebration is a strong signal. It feels good and we know like attracts like. It's a reinforcement of the work you did to co-create that specific manifestation. It's saying, 'We did it, this works! We can do this again, and again, and again.' You must feel your joy when receiving your manifestations. So, when the new house, new job, money, travel, soulmate, health and abundance comes – and it will come – meet it with open arms and let it know just how happy and grateful you are that it's here.

Celebrating our wins is so important because as humans we are naturally driven by rewards. This is especially true when it comes to forming habits: it's hard to stick to a new workout routine until we start feeling stronger and really seeing the results. When new behaviours are followed by positive rewards they are more likely to be repeated until they become habits.

Experiencing your manifestation arrive is a gift in itself, but your commitment to your practice and this new way of being also deserves to be rewarded. So, make time to really acknowledge and celebrate not only your co-creations but also how much you've grown. Reward yourself in any way that feels true.

WAYS TO CELEBRATE YOUR CO-CREATION SUCCESS

Write it down in a gratitude or pride list. There's something powerful about documenting a win on paper. It's a way to record where you began and how you're going. This is the evidence the brain needs to keep momentum and motivation. Repeated practice, learning, and experiences are the keys to building new neural pathways and habits. So go back to your pride and gratitude lists, re-read them, acknowledge all the work it took and see the evidence of your co-creation arriving so your beautiful brain can begin to create the belief that you are a master manifester.

Share it! Tell people about it! Reach out to your co-creation community (more on that soon), or let the friends and family you trust know what you have achieved. Having outside acknowledgement really cements that what you have done is real. That you did this. And that is an important moment of validation that all your hard work, discomfort and sacrifice was worth it.

Symbolise it. I love finding an object that symbolises a co-creation finally arriving. Look for an object that represents your co-creation. It could be a shell you find at a beach after a gratitude meditation for the arrival of your manifestation, or it might be a piece of jewelry that you wear every day that helps remind you of this huge moment and your incredible ability.

I love to make some space for just me (a rarity with two kids), get a bowl of salty potato crisps and a glass of red wine and listen to some music while I reflect on what I have just manifested. Sometimes I will take this reward and celebration out with my friends, toasting to the success of what I have just received and experienced. Some of my friends are also master manifesters, and I am their biggest cheerleader so I love being involved in their reward celebrations too.

It's important to remember that praise and support from others is its own form of reward, and it motivates us to maintain our practice and commitment. This is why it's crucial to have a co-creation community, not only to help support you when times are challenging but also to cheer you on and celebrate your wins.

The Power of Community

When we go through big transitions and rites of passage, we often have to do a lot of the really challenging work ourselves, alone. Many cultures have coming-of-age rituals where an individual is sent off on a quest where they are tested, their power and resilience is pushed to the limit, and they must find the deepest reservoir of inner strength from which to draw. On the other side of these rites of passage, an individual is no longer who they were before. They come back changed, evolved, with new skills and perspectives, abilities and powers. Stronger than before, they then reintegrate with their community.

Co-creation – and all that it asks of you – is your quest. Nobody can do it for you, and because of this it can feel lonely at times. You will be tested, you will be pushed. But I promise it will all fall into place and a time will come when you will realise that you've changed. You are no longer who you were. You have learned how to align yourself with the universe. And then, as with any rite of passage, you'll be ready to return to your community, to offer them support and advice, and receive it in return.

Community is such an important part of co-creation. It is the thing I longed for when I started to do this work; to find and connect with like-minded people who were learning and evolving in real time with me. A community where I could share my questions and my frustrations with honesty and vulnerability. But after waiting twenty years to find a community like this, I got fed up and I created Ariise – the online co-creation community I shared with you in the introduction to his book. Ariise is your place to find your tribe. These are the people who will celebrate your wins, work with you to visualise and prime, hold your hand when you're in the Abyss, and navigate this world of infinite opportunities with you.

One of the greatest gifts this kind of community can offer us is accountability. We all get complacent or lazy at times, especially if we have had great success with manifestation and feel like we have got what we've asked for and things are going our way. And the opposite is also true: something in life can trigger us, maybe even floor us, and leave us feeling like we're starting all over again. Sometimes when we're in pain or feeling anger and frustration, it can seem impossible to continue. And it is in these times we need our community to remind us of the power we have internally to shift our energy, to make the Switch and come back to trust and gratitude.

So, now that you have learned how to co-create the life you truly deserve, I ask you to share what you have discovered with others. Get out there and find your co-creation community!

Epilogue

In the midst of writing this book, something happened that truly tested me and my ability to believe in this work. I went for a routine check-up on my right breast, the one that we'd found a lump in eighteen months earlier. At the time, they had been unable to biopsy it because of the placement of the lump, which meant I had to get an MRI, and then another MRI six months later in order to track the changes to see if there was any growth. As anyone who has ever had to wait on the results of a medical test knows, those six months were awful. And finally, when we got the results back, the lump had shrunk. I felt a little better, but the lump was still there and I knew that I'd have to check it every year for the rest of my life.

At my routine check-up, I was sitting in my specialist's office when she told me that she was concerned: the lump had changed. It felt harder to her. I was confused because it didn't feel harder to me, and I was checking this thing every single day. But she's the expert, so I trusted her gut instinct as well as her medical opinion. We discussed options on the spot, my face giving away how anxious I was. One option was another MRI, and then another period of waiting before checking it again. My doctor explained that she thought there was a 70% chance that I was totally fine. But my interpretation was that there was a 30% chance I had cancer. Memories of my mum's cancer – the loss and the grief and the trauma – immediately flooded me. I tried really hard to stay in that room, but I could feel myself start to dissociate and spiral. Our second option, she told me, was to make a five-centimetre incision on the side of my breast to go in and take the lump out in order to biopsy it.

I told her immediately that I wanted it out. She gave me all of the information about the surgery, the complications and risks, but I was adamant: I wanted this surgery done, and I wanted it done now. My doctor booked me in for four days' time. And the world as I knew it froze: this book, my ambition, all my other work and projects.

I started to spiral. I was thinking about the worst-case scenarios. I called my husband and I told him how things had changed and that I needed surgery and everything felt *big*. Everything felt too much, everything felt unknown. And then I called my best friend Alison, and she just held space for me. She too had lost her mother to breast cancer. She too had had a lump that had needed a biopsy. She too had waited anxiously for results. Alison reminded me that she'd been through this with me before, and she swooped right back in to be with me again. And something happened in that call with her: I clicked back into *this* practice, to co-creation.

The facts were that I had a breast lump which had changed. I was having a surgery we couldn't yet know the outcome of, and we had no control over the result. But I *could* control my reaction. I had let myself spiral into fight-or-flight, into blind panic – all completely normal human responses – but at that moment, I could process the facts. And then I remembered the thing that I walked, talked, preached, practised and lived every single day: trust.

This thing was happening, whether I liked it or not, but stress and spiralling were not going to contribute positively to the experience, or the outcome. I reminded myself that allowing stress hormones and cortisol to take over and send my adrenals firing was not the best state for me to be in before a medical procedure. What my body needed was peace and calm. I anchored myself in what I could control, which was my environment, my immediate circumstances and my support system. And beyond that, all I could do was trust. I anchored myself in the deep trust I have built with my higher power, reminding myself that what is meant for me is for me, and if that meant a breast cancer diagnosis then I had everything I needed to meet that challenge.

I decided that no matter the outcome, I was going to move through it with peace, ease, positivity, understanding, and gratitude for the health care services and specialists I was so lucky to have access to. I paused to feel the deep gratitude I had for Cindy Mak, my breast specialist, for Medicare in Australia, and for health care in general. I shifted out of that spiral into gratitude for what I had and what I *could* do.

I had to wait four days for surgery and another seven days for my results. And throughout this time I felt held and looked after. Something came over me when I decided to trust; a wave of relief and release washed over me. On the day of my surgery (the day after my fortieth birthday), I had actually gone in really excited and grateful, high-spirited and looking forward to a little anaesthetic. That drug they give you just before the anaesthetic is like a glass of champagne!

When it was over, I felt good. I went home and rested. But soon the pain came, and the recovery was much harder than anticipated. I spent an agonising seven days recovering post-treatment and waiting for my check-up and results – agonising not just because of the pain, but because of a conversation I'd had with my son on the day of the surgery. He'd been afraid for me, and I had comforted him. While I didn't tell him all the details, I'd told him the truth about my procedure, that it was to remove a lump.

So he had gone off to school, I'd gone off to surgery. When I got home at about one o'clock and got into bed to rest, still high as a kite on painkillers, my son's school rang and said he'd been feeling off all day. He'd had a sore tummy and he needed us to pick him up. I explained that I had been in surgery, and I'd send my husband up to get him.

As soon as my son came into my bedroom and saw me, the anxiety on his little six-year-old face melted away.

'Have you been feeling sick in the tummy?' I asked.

'Yeah, like lots of butterflies and all these big feelings in my tummy,' he told me.

'I think what you're feeling is something called anxiety,' I said. 'It's a confusing feeling, and sometimes it can feel like being sick.' He said that he felt better now that he could see me; he felt like he could eat and run and play. I felt really glad we were able to help him name the experience he was having. Because I knew when I was going through primary school and I had anxiety, I just felt misunderstood and unwell, and no one was able to help me with that feeling or explain to me how to manage it.

My son went back to school for the rest of the week. But eventually he came back to me two days before my results were due, very late in the evening – which, in my experience, is often when little ones start to really feel whatever they've been masking throughout the day – and said, 'I haven't told you something all week. But I've had anxious all week.'

'Oh darling, why?' I asked.

'Because they cut something out of your boobie. And what if you have to go back in and have more and more cut out? And more and more. And then you've got this really weird boob?'

'Well, who cares what my boob looks like?' I said.

'But you'll look so strange, you won't look like my mum!'

'I'd still look like your mum without a boob,' I told him, but he didn't seem quite convinced.

I comforted him until he felt better and ready to go to sleep. I still had two days of waiting before I'd get my results. The conversation with my son definitely made me shaky; it took me back to how I had felt about my mum's cancer, it took me back to all of the things you cannot control as a child.

I began to wonder not just how I might approach this process, no matter the outcome, but how those around me would approach it too. How were they going to feel? How were they going to experience this? What if it was cancer and I lost my breast or had to get chemo and lose my hair? How would my children process that? I kept oscillating between all of these very heavy, real, human feelings that made me feel out of control, and deep trust in the practice. I truly was in the Abyss. So I did what I know we must do when we're in the Abyss: I visualised peace and positivity. I did everything in my power to co-create a great outcome, even though I was also aware that there was a chance that the universe would have other plans for me – that there might be a divine redirect I would have to accept, surrender to, and deal with if it came. At times like these, there is a great deal of relief to be found in acceptance. I told myself, 'Let go or be dragged', and I trusted the process.

Two days later, it was time to go and see my doctor. When I got to her office I said bluntly: 'I need my results.'

And she said: '*You are healthy.*' She told me that there was no cancer, but that they pulled out six and a half centimetres of tissue. I was relieved, but also once again in a dissociative state, just absorbing the information. I didn't even smile. It took me about a week for the news – *I was okay, I was healthy* – to really land in my body.

And I think that's because I really didn't understand why I was the lucky one. My mum wasn't. My husband's dad wasn't. So many of the most exceptional people I know have not been so lucky. It was hard leaving the cancer clinic knowing that I was okay when so many others inside that building weren't. There were so many mothers of young children facing the worst. This made it feel really unfair that I was okay.

People ask me whether I manifested a positive result. That concept feels disrespectful to my mother and all those who don't get the result they pray for. So, I tell them the truth: that I did my pratice. I trusted. I meditated, journalled, visualised, I anchored myself in gratitude. But no. I don't believe we can manifest life or death, or a positive medical result. We are not God, we are not the universe. We are only human, but we *can* use the incredible practice of co-creation and the grace and trust it allows us to access even in the very darkest times.

Life is incredibly beautiful but there will be hard moments that blindside you, that take you to your knees, that will make you question what it all means. And as much as those times floor us they also make us so much richer, they have the ability to bring clarity to everything. The power of grief transforms us.

I am in awe of people who have experienced real adversity, who have begged for the pain to pass, sobbing into the early hours. To survive this is heroic. Sometimes it is only in experiencing true discomfort that we learn what's necessary to overcome the challenges we face. Resilience, a true sense of self and respect for all things is built by facing the tests life throws at us.

So, if you find yourself here, please know this too shall pass. It will, in fact, make you great. I am saying this as much to you as I am myself. We have come a long way.

I hope you understand now why I say this work is a way of life. It's so much more than co-creation, it's about you. It's giving you access to who you truly are. It's giving you permission to stand in your truth. It's giving you knowledge that has been kept from you. It's urging you to be audacious. This practice wants you to take up space. It wants you to connect with your higher power. It's a reminder of how loved and deserving you are. It's asking you to create the life you deserve.

It's been a gift for me and now, I hope, it's a gift for you.

With deep gratitude,

Zoe

To join the Ariise community, access recordings of
guided meditations and additional resources,
scan the QR code below!

Resources &
Exercises

The Ariise
Co-Creation Checklist

This list is here to help you track your progress as you work on your co-creation goals. You can copy it out into your journal, scan and print it to stick on your mirror, or simply return to this page whenever you need it.

☐ **Find Neutral.** It is only from a place of neutrality, when your nervous system is not in fight-or-flight, that you can move on to the next steps in the process.

☐ **Catalogue your thoughts, core values and beliefs.** Explore how you think and truly feel. What do you really want? Investigate what limiting beliefs might be getting in the way.

☐ **Align your vibe.** Check your vibe. Is it high or low? To align your vibration with a more abundant frequency, work on:
  ● Cultivating an abundant mindset
  ● Finding a state of gratitude
  ● Getting really clear on your goals and desires to ensure they align with your core values
  ● Finding your riisers

☐ **Co-create.** Now you can begin to prepare yourself and your environment to receive your co-creation. This is the part of the process where you are taking aligned action working with the universe. Use the tools available to help you to co-create anything you want. These tools include:
- Meditation
- Affirmations
- Visualisations and priming
- Taking aligned action
- Rituals
- Storytelling and re-parenting your inner child
- Pride lists
- Micro-manifesting
- The Switch

☐ **Break through the blocks.** Understand the purpose of tests and the Abyss and be prepared to confront any worries and doubts that you may face. This is a natural part of the process.

☐ **Receive and accept.** You have done the work and now it's time to trust the process as you prepare to receive and accept. When your manifestations arrive:
- Record your success with pride and gratitude lists
- Celebrate your wins
- Share your success with your co-creation community

☐ **Maintain your momentum.** Keep that momentum going by focusing on your next co-creation.

Zoe's Recommended Reading List

Conversations with God

by Neale Donald Walsch

Key takeaway: Conversations with God offers a perspective on the divine and the laws of the universe that can help shift your approach to manifestation.

You Can Heal Your Life

by Louise Hay

Key takeaway: This book provides deep insight into how our beliefs impact our health and prosperity and offers tools for self-healing.

The Power of Now

by Eckhart Tolle

Key takeaway: Tolle's teachings emphasise living in the present moment, which is essential for successful co-creation.

Atomic Habits

by James Clear

Key takeaway: Clear offers a practical guide to building good habits into everyday life—perfect for supporting your co-creation practice.

Untamed

by Glennon Doyle

Key takeaway: In this inspiring memoir, Doyle shares her story of moving away from people-pleasing to discover a more authentic 'untamed' self. It's all about setting boundaries and being real.

Big Magic

by Elizabeth Gilbert

Key takeaway: This book looks at how we can live more creative and fulfilling lives – by letting go of fear, self-doubt and perfectionism.

The Four Agreements

by Don Miguel Ruiz

Key takeaway: Ruiz teaches four principles for cultivating a mindset that will bring peace and empowerment to your life.

Daring Greatly

by Brené Brown

Key takeaway: As a psychologist, Brown knows how transformative being vulnerable and open can be. This book teaches you that opening up emotionally can build courage, connection and even creativity.

The Intuition Handbook

by Joel Pearson

Key takeaway: Pearson explores the neuroscience behind the idea of intuition, arguing that it is a powerful tool we can harness in everyday life. The book includes practical exercises for enhancing your intuition.

Ask and It Is Given

by Esther and Jerry Hicks

Key takeaway: This book is all about the Law of Attraction and how positive thinking can help us shape a brighter future for ourselves.

The Power of Intention

by Dr Wayne Dyer

Key takeaway: Dyer explores how deepening our connection with our inner selves can help us let go of limiting beliefs and harness the power of intention.

Limiting Beliefs Worksheet

1. What is the limiting belief? It could be something like 'I lack self-discipline' or 'I am unlovable'.

    _____

    _____

2. Where did it come from? Did you learn it from a parent, a peer, a teacher?

    _____

    _____

3. When did it start?

    _____

    _____

4. What evidence do you have that this belief is true?

    _____

    _____

    _____

    _____

    _____

5. What evidence do you have that it this belief is false?

_____

_____

_____

_____

_____

6. Find the opposite of your limiting belief and write it down. This might look like changing 'I'm unlovable' to 'I am surrounded by people who love and support me'.

_____

_____

7. Now expand on this idea by listing some evidence to support this belief. This could be, 'I'm so loveable, I can list three friends who really care about me and love spending time with me'.

_____

_____

8. Write down an aligned action you intend to take to embody this new belief. For example, 'I will reach out to my friends to organise a dinner party'.

_____

_____

Setting Boundaries Worksheet

1. What are the areas in your life where you feel that you need to set firmer boundaries? Consider your social life, family commitments, the workplace and particular relationships.

   _____

   _____

   _____

   _____

2. Think of a time in your life where your boundaries have been crossed. How did you respond?

   _____

   _____

   _____

   _____

   _____

   _____

   _____

3. How did that make you feel?

_____

_____

_____

_____

_____

_____

_____

4. How would you have liked to respond instead?

_____

_____

_____

_____

_____

_____

_____

5. How do you think responding in this *new* way would make you feel?

_____

_____

_____

_____

_____

_____

_____

6. Reflecting on your communication style, what would you need to work on to be able to respond in the way you have outlined above? Is it self-confidence or assertiveness? Is it being prepared in advance?

_____

_____

_____

_____

_____

_____

_____

7. List three things you can implement today that will help you enforce your boundaries with kindness and compassion in future.

_____

_____

_____

_____

_____

_____

_____

Boundary Mapping Exercise

STEP ONE

Begin by drawing a simple outline of yourself on a piece of paper. It doesn't need to be perfect, just a basic representation.

STEP TWO

Imagine a bubble around yourself, symbolising your personal space and your boundaries, both physically and emotionally. Now draw this bubble around your self-portrait.

STEP THREE

In the space outside the bubble, write down or draw symbols to represent some of the things you'd like to establish boundaries around.

STEP FOUR

Inside your bubble, write down or draw some of the benefits you will welcome into your life by establishing these boundaries. These might include things like time for self-care, peace and calm, or happier relationships.

STEP FIVE

Take a moment to reflect on why establishing each boundary is important to you, and the benefits you will see once you enforce it. Keep your drawing as a powerful visual reminder that you are creating space for yourself.

Pride List

I am proud of . . .

1.

2.

3.

4.

5.

Gratitude list

I am grateful for . . .

1.

2.

3.

4.

5.

Goal Setting

Goals for this month . . .

1.

2.

3.

What will help me achieve them is . . .

_____

_____

_____

_____

_____

_____

Goals for this year . . .

1.

2.

3.

What will help me achieve them is . . .

_____

_____

_____

_____

_____

_____

Goals for five years from now . . .

1.

2.

3.

What will help me achieve them is . . .

_____

_____

_____

Journalling Prompts

To me, true happiness looks like . . .

_____

_____

_____

_____

_____

_____

_____

_____

_____

_____

_____

_____

_____

_____

_____

_____

_____

_____

I feel free when I am . . .

_____

_____

_____

_____

_____

_____

_____

_____

_____

_____

_____

_____

_____

_____

_____

_____

_____

_____

_____

I want . . .

_____

_____

_____

_____

_____

_____

_____

_____

And I want it because . . .

_____

_____

_____

_____

_____

_____

_____

_____

_____

_____

I am deserving of what I desire because . . .

_____

_____

_____

_____

_____

_____

_____

_____

_____

_____

_____

_____

_____

_____

_____

_____

_____

_____

_____

_____

I am being held back by . . .

_____

_____

_____

_____

_____

_____

_____

_____

_____

_____

_____

_____

_____

_____

_____

_____

_____

_____

_____

_____

I need to let go of . . .

_____

_____

_____

And when I do I will feel . . .

_____

_____

_____

_____

_____

_____

_____

_____

_____

_____

_____

_____

_____

_____

_____

A habit I need to break is . . .

_____

_____

_____

The positive outcomes of breaking this habit will be . . .

_____

_____

_____

_____

_____

_____

_____

_____

_____

_____

_____

_____

_____

_____

_____

_____

_____

I will set boundaries around . . .

_____

_____

_____

_____

_____

_____

_____

_____

_____

_____

_____

_____

_____

_____

_____

_____

_____

_____

_____

_____

The things I like most about myself are . . .

_____

_____

_____

_____

_____

_____

_____

_____

_____

_____

_____

_____

_____

_____

_____

_____

_____

_____

_____

_____

_____

Acknowledgements

I was very naive when I agreed to write this book. I had a very romanticised vision of this experience. As much as its a labour of love and something I am immensly proud of, it was not easy. I needed a village to support me in creating this book.

Firstly, thank you to my wonderful team at Simon & Schuster. Emma, you saw something in me years ago when I wasn't ready or prepared to write. And you were so open and willing when I was. I hope this book surprises you, because I think it's so much more than we both thought it could be. Lizzie, we have had some very interesting moments together. We both know it had to be right, it had to be truthful. It is. And Naima: What a process! Thank you for being a gentle, soft and loving guide. Thank you for all the care and support and hours and hours of time spent bringing this book to life.

Flex, you cracked me wide open at a pivotal part of this process. Both personally and through your insights on the book. You have this incredible ability to see me. This wisdom you imparted was profoundly important to this process. Thank you for saying the hard things that I know are never hard between us. I remember the day I manifested you into my life. I was giddy, like a girl that just fell in love. You are a sister now. Thank you for your beautiful mind and your willingness to go deep. We all benefit so much from you being in the world.

Thank you Nina, for always encouraging me to write. For always believing in me. You said my words were beautiful even when they felt silly and rudimentary to me. I didn't believe I could take up space as a writer. When you read this book, you were excited, gentle and wise. The notes, the feedback, the reasons why were so anchored in love and had such thought and impact behind them. I took every single one of them to heart. Your opinion means more to me than anyone. You are a true riiser for me and so many: the books, the work, the impact you are making on the world astounds me and I will forever be grateful for our thirty-six years of friendship.

To my dear friend, Alison Rice: thank you for holding me when no one else knew how to. What more can I say?

Annie, when my mum asked you to be my godmother, it's as if she knew I would need you through some of the hardest parts of my life. You have turned up for me and my family consistently and without question. You are the most incredible 'Annie Annie' to my kids and I am so grateful for all your love and support throughout my life.

Benji – thank you for being the greatest human I have ever met. You are a true riiser for so many, and for me. Your generosity, your support and your unwavering belief in me has allowed me to feel safe to write the words I have in this book. I am forever grateful to you and to us. What a gift this love is.

To my children, Ever and Fox, thank you for being the greatest teachers. I love how wise and truthful you are. I appreciate how you are a mirror for me, especially now through my next evolution of self, you unknowingly show me the shadows of myself.

When I see little you, I see little me. I get to witness what healthy attachment styles look like in real time and what a wonderful dependable father–child relationship looks like. It is deeply healing. Benji, we broke the generational trauma.

And finally, to Mum – I could feel you the whole time I was writing. What I would do to have one last long, warm hug. The longing for you will never cease; what a beautiful yet tragic love story we had. Thank you for raising me with the openness to receive this work. You showed me the epitome of unconditional love.

About the Author

Zoe is a seasoned media professional with over 15 years of experience, including hosting radio and TV shows in New Zealand and Australia, writing newspaper columns, and creating content for renowned brands. She's the creator of three acclaimed podcast brands: *Ariise*, *The Deep* and its subscription counterpart, *Deeper*.

Her international award-winning podcast *The Deep* has captivated audiences with its powerful storytelling, reaching the Top 10 on the Apple charts within two weeks and achieving a five-day stint at Number 1. Zoe is celebrated for her talent in making guests feel at ease, enabling candid conversations with a diverse range of individuals, from those facing terminal diagnoses to conscious sex workers.

Alongside her media career, Zoe is married to NRL legend Benji Marshall and a devoted mother to their children, Fox and Ever. Amidst a dynamic career, she has embraced motherhood with passion and joy.